D1524759

ASO

J. Ranade IBM Series

ASO

Automated Systems Operations for MVS

Trevor Eddolls

McGraw-Hill, Inc.

New York St. Louis San Francisco Auckland Bogotá
Caracas Lisbon London Madrid Mexico Milan
Montreal New Delhi Paris San Juan São Paulo
Singapore Sydney Tokyo Toronto

Library of Congress Cataloging-in-Publication Data

Eddolls, Trevor.
    ASO : automated systems operations for MVS / Trevor Eddolls.
        p.   cm.
    Includes index.
    ISBN 0-07-018994-3
    1. Management information systems.   2. IBM MVS.   I. Title.
T58.64.E38   1992
005.4'429—dc20   92-28693
                                                                      CIP

*This book is dedicated to
Jill, Katy, and Jennifer*

1 2 3 4 5 6 7 8 9 0   DOC/DOC   9 8 7 6 5 4 3 2

ISBN   0-07-018994-3

*The sponsoring editor for this book was Jerry Papke, the editing
supervisor was Fred Dahl, and the production supervisor was Pamela
A. Pelton. It was set in Century Schoolbook by Inkwell Publishing
Services.*

Printed and bound by R. R. Donnelley & Sons Company.

Contents

Preface

It has been estimated that there are over 15,000 licenses of IBM's flagship operating system MVS (Multiple Virtual Storage) throughout the world, which makes it a huge marketplace for vendors of software that runs under MVS.

MVS sites can be divided into those using:

MVS/SP Version 1, which still uses the old 24-bit addressing.

MVS/XA sites (MVS/SP Version 2), which makes use of 31-bit addressing giving 2 GB address spaces, and channel paths.

MVS/ESA users (MVS/SP Version 3 and Version 4), which provides hiperspaces and dataspaces as a way of improving performance.

When referring to MVS sites, this book usually means XA and ESA sites.

IBM's other operating systems are VSE (Virtual Storage Extended) and VM. These operating systems are each in use at more sites than MVS is, but the sites tend to be smaller and tend to make lower demands on the system in terms of performance.

MVS is typically used at larger sites that require high performance and that carry large volumes of work. These sites are the ones that look to automation as a way of improving the performance of the system and improving the service offered to end users.

This book not only examines ways of automating the many aspects of MVS, but also examines how the work of network operators can be automated and generally how automation can be used at remote sites.

This book is written for all people who are to be involved with automation at a site. It contains details of the areas that can be automated (e.g., the console) and the way that the automation can be carried out, which is of particular interest to operators, database administrators, and systems programmers. It contains information about the benefits that can be derived from automation and the costs involved, which would be of special interest to management. It also contains examples showing how the end user's way of working will change because of the automation software, which will be of special interest to end users.

In a recent survey, it was found that many sites considered automation to involve nothing more than automating the console. While this book covers this area thoroughly, it also looks at other areas that can be automated, such as scheduling and printing, and describes what can be done to bring about fully automated systems operations.

Although the book is aimed primarily at MVS sites, the principles involved apply to sites running other operating systems. The book also illustrates how automated systems operations at an MVS site can be extended to cover automation and control of other platforms, such as DEC, Hewlett-Packard, and other mainframes. Additionally, it looks at the importance of extending the automation from mainframe to PCs and workstations attached to the mainframe.

Many products are mentioned in the text and listed in the appendices. These names are copyrighted by the supplier. The products that are mentioned are used as illustrations of those available in a particular area, and no recommendation for any one company's products is made explicitly or implicitly. Anyone selecting a product should check that it meets their requirements rather than relying on the fact that the product is mentioned in the text.

Acknowledgments

I would like to thank all the people who have been prepared to give their opinion on operators and the way that the work of the operations group could be improved. And I would like to thank all the operators I used to work with for showing me what being an operator is really like.

I would also like to take this opportunity to thank the people at Xephon plc who offered helpful advice about what automated systems operations meant to management and end users, and who also helped with the research for this book.

No book would be complete without a special thank you to my family for their help and encouragement. Therefore I would like to express my appreciation to Jill, my wife, and Katy and Jennifer, my daughters.

Finally I would like to mention my Mum and Dad; and also Jan, Tracey, and Emma Phillips who, although they didn't help with this book, wanted to see their names in it anyway.

Trevor Eddolls

1

Introduction

In order for a company to be competitive, it needs to be getting the best work it can from its employees. This often means getting results or information quickly—more quickly than competitive companies can get the same results or information. It is the end user, in computer terms, who needs to get the results and information from the computer as quickly and as easily as possible.

To the end user, the computer is a tool. It is not endlessly fascinating in its own right; it is just another tool to use to get the job done fast and efficiently. The end user does not necessarily want to know how to code programs in COBOL, how to write JCL (Job Control Language), or the importance of LU6.2. The end user wants to sit at a screen, tell the machine what information is needed, and read the results back from the screen in seconds.

The end user wants to be able to sit at a 3278, a PC (personal computer), or any other terminal and be able to work without having to know a number of arcane commands. The end user does not want to have to phone people to ask if they will write the JCL for a job that should run tonight; they do not want to phone someone to include their job in a schedule, they do not want to have to get pieces of paper signed by their manager to be taken to somebody else's manager before their work can take place. They also don't want to know if the mainframe is located in the next room or on a different continent. The end user expects computer services to be available all day and every day.

The MIS (management information systems) department is responsible for providing the computer service used by these people. The MIS department is part of the company, and for the company to be successful the MIS department must be successful. The MIS department must realize that it is offering a service to the company, and, if it fails to offer the right kind of service, there might be no company left to have an MIS department.

One of the ways many companies see that a better service can be offered by the MIS department is through automation. The idea is to automate as much of the operation of the system as possible. This is what is known as *automated systems operations* (ASO). In many peoples' minds automation is no longer a luxury; it is a necessary business requirement.

Automated systems operations should not be considered an end in itself. Its principal aim is to allow the MIS department to offer a better service to its users so that those users can help the company compete more successfully in business. The automation should be part of the company's policy for the company's future growth and success. In fact, the automated systems operations strategy adopted must reflect both the short-term and long-term commercial requirements of a company.

When introducing automated systems operations, it is better to concentrate on improvements in quality rather than improvements in productivity. This is because productivity improvements will result from the improved quality.

Initially, automation of the operator's role was considered all that was necessary in terms of automated systems operations, and much has been written about automated operations (AO). Indeed, much of the initial work carried out at a site on the road to automated systems operations will be by its very nature AO. But for MVS sites in particular, this is now only part of the story. IBM has introduced SMS (System Managed Storage) as a concept with associated products that will automate the way that files and disks are managed. IBM has also given us SystemView (September 1990 announcements) which while not being a product—or an architecture for that matter—gives us a view of how IBM sees data center structure evolving, and that concept involves a high degree of automation. Also, many sites are looking to automated systems operations as a way of automating and controlling multiple platforms (e.g., DEC or Hewlett-Packard machines as well) from a single control point.

At every stage in the processing of work on the computer where a human being is involved, there is an opportunity for a mistake to be made. Automated systems operations is an attempt to reduce these "opportunities" to a minimum by passing control of systems to software, and thereby reducing the number of potential problems and improving performance, efficiency, and the service provided to end users.

In the traditional mainframe installation, one or more large computers were kept in their own room. Access to the computer consoles and other devices was restricted to operators, systems programmers, and engineers. In the early days, large numbers of operators were required to service the needs of the machine. They would feed in paper tape or card decks; they would collect punched cards, and put multiline or special stationery on the printer. They would also be required to change removal disks on 3330s or 3340s and load reel-to-reel tapes on magnetic tape drives.

The operators would also be required to power on or off the hardware and IML (Initial Microcode Load) and IPL (Initial Program Load) the processor. While the machine was running, operators would stand by the console responding to messages displayed, and would be responsible for starting and stopping batch jobs, changing the priority of jobs, and routing output to the appropriate printers. They would also be called upon to recover the system and subsystems in the event of a crash.

As various departments within the company were computerized, the amount of work for operators to do was increased. As the latest hardware developments were installed, the amount of work that the operator had to perform was reduced while, at the same time, the amount of information the operator was required to know increased. The net result is that the number of staff required is lower than in earlier times. Most companies are now considering that, if every other department is computerized, it must be time to computerize the computer department, i.e., to automate systems operations.

However, many sites are finding that their earliest attempts at automation do not fit well together. In the days before automated operations was a fashionable concept, some degree of automation had been taking place. The reasons for automating were, as with most things, to improve performance and service levels, etc. The products that were available were initially stand-alone products with no thought given to integration with other automation products. The types of software products available could be used for scheduling batch work and performance monitoring. Nowadays, it is necessary to look at the larger automation picture when planning which products to implement.

Sites must realize that, when implementing automated systems operations, it is not enough simply to automate existing procedures, it is an opportunity to introduce new improved procedures. It is important to remember that the automation will not take place over night and that, in the period while the automation is taking place, the environment itself will be changing. New hardware or new software may be introduced and installed. There may also be changes in the business, e.g., taking over another company, increases in production of one type of component, etc. Therefore, when planning the automation, this "moving goal post" scenario must be borne in mind, and a degree of flexibility must be built into the plan.

The introduction of automated systems operations means that the operator's expertise—and to a degree that of the system programmer, data administrator, JCL writer—is moved into the automation tools, and manual work is given back to the end users who want their tasks performed. The end users become responsible for their own activities. With fewer trained operators generally available, automated systems operations offers management an escape route from the operations skill shortage.

The automation of operator functions is usually a two-stage process. In the first stage, operators are expected to be present and the automation is designed to make their job easier. It involves suppression of some of the messages that appear on the console, it involves automatically starting jobs at the right time, it involves presenting colorful displays from monitor software so that the operator can see whether or not everything is working perfectly.

In the second stage, the operator is not expected to be present. The software is meant to perform all the functions that would previously have been performed by an operator, and only when it cannot cope will it contact someone to come and solve whatever problem it has identified. There is usually a slow migration from stage one to stage two.

Automated systems operations software must be modular. If one part crashes, it must not bring down the whole automation system. Anyone managing the introduction of the automation software must have a contingency plan for what to do in the event of the automation software itself abending.

This book is written primarily for sites using IBM's MVS (multiple virtual storage) operating system as their main operating system, although parallels could easily be drawn by users of other mainframe computers and operating systems. The book's aims are to show what is meant by automated systems operations, what can be achieved, what difficulties have to be overcome, and to illustrate ways that can be used to achieve fully automated systems operations. The book details all the areas associated with system operations and describes the choices available to reduce human activity, improve service, and automate each of those areas.

Chapter 2 discusses what is meant by automated systems operations. It also describes what is meant by various terms used in connection with automated operations, such as lights-out operation, bridge operation, and unattended operations.

Chapter 3 looks at why there is a need for automated systems operations at computer sites. It looks at the economic, technological, and cultural pressure being put on the MIS department.

Chapter 4 reviews the benefits to a company of moving towards automated systems operations. These benefits are discussed in some detail.

Chapter 5 takes the lid off the downside of automated systems operations. It goes through the costs that will be incurred if an automation policy is adopted. Initial expenditure, running costs, and hidden outgoing cash flows are described.

Very few things in life are straightforward, and the introduction of automated systems operations is no exception. Chapter 6 is devoted to looking at the difficulties that have to be overcome before ASO can be fully implemented.

Probably the biggest problem that a site will face with the introduction of ASO is the reluctance or downright opposition to it from people. Chapter 7 looks at some of the reasons people may give for not wanting ASO and suggests ways that people can be encouraged to adopt the policy for the good of all.

Chapter 8 looks at how to carry out the automation. It lists, from a management point of view, the steps that have to be taken for a successful implementation of ASO. It covers areas such as selecting the project team and defining installation policy. What areas the project team needs to look at are discussed, including what areas of human involvement with the computer currently exist and how this involvement can be eliminated. Automation software requirements are described, as are the stages that are usually gone through in the final implementation.

Chapter 9 reviews the hardware that is currently available to take away the need for human interaction. Alternatives to tape usage are described, and new facilities associated with processors to ensure system stability and removing the need to re-IPL are discussed. Part of the chapter also looks at the benefits to automated systems operations of using PCs.

In a recent survey, many sites considered message suppression to be all there was to automated operations. Chapter 10 not only looks at what can be done with messages (suppression, rewording so that text is meaningful, and automatic answering), but also looks at other aspects of console-related operator activity that can be automated (starting and stopping subsystems at the appropriate time, investigating system status before answering messages, issuing query commands to monitor system components).

Printing is an activity that in the past has taken up much of the operator's time. Chapter 11 looks at ways that printing can be eliminated, or performed automatically when it cannot be eliminated. It also looks at what report distribution system software can do.

Chapter 12 examines schedulers and how they fit into an automated systems operations environment. The benefits of using a scheduler are explored, and the facilities that schedulers should offer are also discussed. Associated software is briefly examined: software to ensure that the right procedure is used and the procedure points to the right program which is in the right program library, and software to ensure that there is enough disk space before a file is written to disk.

Traditionally batch run balancing has been carried out in the evening by operators. Totals from one piece of output have been checked against other totals. If all is satisfactory, the next job is started. In the past, errors have occurred costing a company money in lost time and reruns. Chapter 13 looks at ways to remove the human involvement in checking batch totals.

Once the automation system is in place and people are removed, what happens when something goes wrong? Chapter 14 examines what happens when a failure occurs with the following: application programs, subsystems, the operating system, hardware, the network, the automation system, and the automated problem management system. It also suggests ways round the problems.

CICS (Customer Information Control System) is a very popular transaction processing system. Many end users are connected to CICS and are dependent on its performing well for the success of their work. Chapter 15 looks at ways that CICS can be automated and briefly describes some of the new tools from IBM.

Most MVS sites have at least one monitor package. The introduction of automated systems operations allows the monitor to be linked to the automation software so that it not only clearly shows a problem to the operator, but also takes steps to remove the problem or even prevents the problem from occurring. This is described in Chapter 16.

Chapter 17 looks at network operation and how it can be automated.

Chapter 18 describes IBM's NetView. MVS sites can run at least two copies of NetView. One can look after communications, and be linked to VTAM. The other can be used in automated systems operations. This chapter looks at both aspects of NetView.

Chapter 19 looks at remote operations, which can be used to control a mainframe by operators at a distant site. It can also be used to allow an operator to dial in from a PC and perform operator type activities in circumstances where no one is on site to operate the mainframe.

September 1990 saw the announcement of SystemView by IBM. This announcement showed the direction that IBM was thinking data center evolution was going. SystemView is important to anyone preparing an automated systems operations policy, and some of the SystemView tools now available can be used as part of an automation policy. This is discussed in Chapter 20.

Chapter 21 looks at the ways automation can be used in relation to storage management. There are two main areas discussed: System Managed Storage (SMS) and the Information Warehouse framework.

Many sites planning automation know that some messages or situations occur so rarely that it is almost impossible to set up the automation software to deal with them. In these circumstances, and even earlier if they know what they are doing, sites can make use of an expert system. Chapter 22 looks at what is involved in using an expert system.

Without operators, end users experiencing difficulties have to contact someone else to help them. Chapter 23 looks at the role of the Help Desk in an automated systems operations environment, describing the benefits associated with having one and the way it should operate.

Chapter 24 looks at Service Level Agreements (SLAs) and asset management. With the introduction of automation it is necessary to ensure that the service to end users is maintained. SLAs are a way of doing that. With fewer people around, knowing what hardware and software is available and in use at a site needs to be automated. The process of changing anything needs to be automated. This is also found in Chapter 24.

Chapter 25 describes why an automation audit is necessary and how to perform it.

Controlling access to data and hardware is important at all times. With the introduction of automation, its importance increases. Chapter 26 looks at ASO and security.

Chapter 27 discusses how to manage an ASO environment. It describes how to manage the introduction of ASO and how to manage things once ASO is running.

Chapter 28 offers a view of what the future holds for sites in terms of ASO. Even as this chapter was being written, companies were announcing software that would perform some aspects of the future scenario described.

Appendix A lists some of the questions that a site could ask a software company to help in the selection of their automation software package.

Appendix B lists a number of automation packages that run under MVS, along with the suppliers' names and addresses.

Anyone who is about to embark on the automation of their system could do worse than bear in mind the words of Niccolo Machiavelli.

> There is nothing more difficult to plan, more doubtful of success, nor more dangerous to manage than the creation of a new system. For the initiator has the enmity of all who would profit from the preservation of the old system and merely lukewarm defenders in those who would gain by the new one. *The Prince*, 1513.

2

Automated Systems Operations—What It Is

The ultimate goal of automated systems operations is to remove all human intervention in the way the computer works with the exception of the end user, perhaps the engineer, and, of course, the person who tells the automation software what rules to follow. Figure 2.1 shows what many people wrongly consider to be the final role for humans in an automated systems operations environment.

Automated systems operations can be defined as a way of letting the hardware and/or the software perform MIS-related activities that previously required human intervention.

Automated systems operations can be thought of as the process by which the computer center is computerized. This means that hardware and software are used to perform the work previously carried out by humans.

For end users, life becomes much less complicated with the introduction of automated systems operations. End users need to know even less about what is going on behind the scenes. They can request an action to be carried out on the computer, and it will be performed by the automation software without the need for human involvement.

Automated systems operations has recently gained in popularity mainly because it offers a way to simplify and unify the operation of a complex computer environment.

MIS departments are always expected to deal with more information better and faster than ever before. However, the MIS department faces its own problems, such as budget constraints, availability/service levels, and perception of response. MIS is continually expected to do more with less, and do it better. Automated systems operations offers a way to overcome these problems.

Figure 2.1. Automated systems operations.

Automated systems operations can be expanded from simple control of the MVS operating system to control of other IBM operating systems [e.g., VM (Virtual Machine) and VSE (Virtual Storage Extended)] and also operating systems on hardware supplied by, for example, DEC or Hewlett-Packard.

Automated systems operations also applies to users of PCs and workstations that are attached to the mainframe across a LAN (local area network) or WAN (wide area network). Versions of application software in use on the PCs and back-ups of user files can all be regulated and controlled by automated systems operations.

At the heart of every MIS department is at least one mainframe. Connected to this mainframe are a number of peripheral devices, such as tape drives, printers, and in the past card readers and removable disks. These peripherals have required the intervention of humans, called operators. The initial thrust of automated system operations is typically automated operations. The main idea permeating automated operations is that the role of the operator is automated, that is, wherever possible the machine does the job. Automated systems operations takes this idea and extends it to include many other computer-related areas that usually involve some kind of human intervention. Automated systems operations can be thought to include, in addition to the activities of operators, the activities of:

File managers, those people responsible for the placement of files on disk and the back-up of those files.

Database administrators, who have a similar role but associated with proprietary databases (e.g., DB2).

Data entry staff.

Media distributors.

JCL writers, schedulers.

Systems programmers.

Performance management is another area that can benefit from automated systems operations. If a system problem occurs, nowadays, not only are there fewer systems programmers who can read a system dump, dumps now tend to be so large that it is very time consuming trying to identify a problem. Also, most sites cannot afford to keep the system down while the systems programmer pores over the dump. It is more efficient to let the software identify the problem and overcome it. An example of software that can be used in this role is AF/Performer from Candle. Candle's Omegaview, part of their Omegacenter, identifies failing components, and AF/Performer, using a set of rule-based applications, fixes them.

Automated Operations

The automation of the operators role can be carried out to varying degrees, and these are usually categorized as:

- Lights-dim operation.
- Lights-out operation.
- Bridge operation.
- Remote operation.
- Unattended operations.

Lights-dim operation

The concept behind lights-dim operation is simple enough. It assumes that operators are still a necessary prerequisite for the satisfactory running of the computer, but their presence is required only some of the time. It is considered by many as a halfway house between operations with people around the computer, and full lights-out operation.

With the increase in power of computers, and the increase in the number of jobs that can pass through them in a given time, it seems most likely that this will become not so much a halfway house, as the final stage for many sites. The majority of operators will work social hours only and perform a much more skilled role during that time. Most people consider it unlikely that all operators can ever be completely dispensed with, although their role may change or their job function may be integrated into another job.

Lights-out operation

To complicate matters, lights-out operation is used to refer to two slightly different concepts. It can refer to lights-out by location or lights-out by time.

Lights-out by location. Lights-out by location refers to the isolation of certain pieces of hardware in an area that the operators do not have to enter in the normal course of events. The room does not need to be illuminated because no one needs to see anything. Therefore, it is called a dark room, and the operation of that room is considered lights-out. The type of equipment that could be moved into such a room includes:

- The processor itself.
- DASD (direct access storage device).
- Front-end processors or communication controllers.

Currently, a number of companies that have computer sites at a number of different locations run most of them as lights-out environments. Only one or perhaps two sites have operators, and these sites control the others.

Lights-out by time. An alternative approach to lights-out operation is to turn out the lights in an ordinary computer room for certain periods of time. This might be overnight or on weekends when operators would not wish to be on shift. The net result of this is that no functions requiring operator intervention can take place, and any failures that cannot be dealt with by software have to wait until the operations staff returns before they are dealt with.

Bridge operations

Bridge operation can in many ways be thought of as the same as the first example of lights-out operation. While most of the computer room is kept free of operators, an area is set aside which is like the bridge of a ship. In this area, the system console, the MVS console, the VTAM (virtual telecommunications access method) console, the CICS master terminal, and any other necessary screens are placed together, and the operators remain here almost all the time, monitoring and controlling what happens on the computer and the network. The bridge can be used to control multiple platforms located at various sites round the world.

Remote operations

With the improvements in software and the greater reliability of communication links, it is possible for operators at one physical location to control the workings of another computer at a location many miles away. All messages would be routed from one computer to the other, and the operators could then perform all the necessary activities to ensure that all the computers under their care function properly. A number of companies are running most of their computer sites from a single site. The other sites can run lights-out.

An extension to this idea is where the operator dials into the mainframe from a remote PC. He can communicate with the automation software to see if he is needed on site. He could, using the PC, answer any outstanding messages or give the automation software any special instructions. He can then log off until a later time. If the operator has a pager, the automation software can page him in the event of a problem. The operator can log on and solve the problem. This method allows operations staff to be off site overnight and during holiday periods.

Unattended operations

The idea behind unattended operations is that there are no operators at all to pay attention to the mainframe. This means that all functions previously performed by operators should be carried out by software or by the end user. The software would control the flow of work through the processor. The end user would be responsible for submitting jobs and printing output. Printers would be near the end user, not the mainframe.

Automated operations—present and future

Most sites are treating the introduction of automated operations as an opportunity to improve the service offered by the MIS department to the end users. They are, typically, not taking steps to remove all their operators. To automate to such an extent that no operator is required at any time is, for most sites, a way off in the future.

A typical site is using AO as an opportunity to make life easier for the operators so that they are not continually working under pressure and will not therefore make so many mistakes. In this way, the operations department can offer a better service to the end users.

3

Automated Systems Operations— Why It Is Needed

Automated systems operations is needed at the majority of sites for two reasons. The first is that there are enormous financial benefits available to sites that move to automated systems operations. The second is that fewer mistakes will be made and the level of service offered will be improved.

Most computer sites, nowadays, are working under pressure. Some of the pressures on a site currently include:

- An increase in complexity of the hardware, architecture(s), and operating systems. It is getting to the stage where things are almost too complex for a single person to understand all of them. The cost to a company of errors can be very high.

- An increase in the performance requirements of end users.

- An increase in workload because more people are using the computer services, and are expecting more from them

- An increase in the specialization of support staff, along with an increase in the number of support staff required.

Another pressure is the recession, which is focusing companies on the need to make money and cut computing costs/head counts.

An automation policy can help to better position a site for future changes including new machine platforms, client-server growth, and the increased use of workstations.

Automated systems operations is considered by many to be one of the most successful weapons in their armory when it comes to increasing business efficiency. This can be the difference between a company with a future in these competitive times, and one with only a history. Automated systems operations can be thought of as increasing the efficiency and effectiveness of the computer and all the people who use it, and also of increasing the job satisfaction of those associated with it. The introduction of automated systems operations allows an even more complex data center environment to be introduced in the future. (A full list of the benefits that can result from automated systems operations is given in Chap. 4.)

Different sites will have different reasons for moving towards automated systems operations, and different sites may assign different weights to the same reason. The reasons can usually be divided into economic pressure, technological pressure, and cultural pressure.

There is one other reason that I have heard put forward for moving to automated systems operations and this is the "lemming theory." The lemming theory states that, if enough people either are doing something or appear to be doing something, then almost everyone else will also want to do the same thing, irrespective of the potential benefits or costs.

Economic Pressure

The most frequent economic need given for moving to automated systems operations is the need to improve operations' performance. Many companies are moving completely away from the idea that MIS is a maverick department allowed to make its own demands on the company and in general to go its own way, absorbing whatever sums of money it decides are necessary. Typically, in today's economic climate, companies have a business plan and the MIS department has to fit into that business plan. In fact, the MIS department is an essential element in that plan, and the performance of the MIS department is crucial to the success of the company as a whole.

A necessary consequence of this is that the work of the operators comes under close scrutiny. Management is likely to be receptive to any ideas or suggestions of ways that improvements in performance could be made, and managers will most likely ensure that the suggestions are implemented. A consequence of this is to move to automated systems operations.

The economic pressures can be summarized as:

- MIS budget.
- Policy of reducing head counts.
- Increased cost of employing skilled staff.
- Increased cost of downtime—caused by operators.
- Improved hardware reliability.
- Need to improve image by improving service.
- Trend to decentralization.

At most sites during recessionary periods there is a reduction in the amount of money available to spend, and each department has to fully justify the use of every penny allocated. This reduction in the MIS budget is putting pressure on the MIS management.

People are usually the largest cost for a company. Every year the price of a megabyte of storage comes down, but the cost of employing one human being goes up. Therefore, savings can be made if automation software does the work rather than people, and the number of people employed is reduced.

The cost of employing skilled people is rising faster than the cost of unskilled people. The more that members of staff know and can do, the better placed they are to get a higher-paying job elsewhere. Higher salaries have to be paid to retain them and their skill. These extra payments are no longer necessary if the software contains the expertise of the people.

The period during which end users cannot make use of the computer is a period during which they are unproductive. This means that the company is losing the work that end users could be performing. Many system and subsystem outages are caused by operator error. If operators are replaced by software, these errors will not take place. When operators restart systems and subsystems, they read messages before responding to them, and the restart takes place at human speed. With automation, restarts take place at machine speed and the system is back for end users much faster.

Newer hardware is more reliable than ever before. It is not necessary to have operators minding the equipment to nurse jobs through. The hardware can perform more reliably and much faster.

Many sites can tell the most appalling stories of catastrophes and the cause of the drama is usually placed squarely on the operators. Many sites have made it a habit to think of operators as unthinking louts. This stereotyping tends to cloud people's perceptions of the service offered by the MIS department. The move to automation is an opportunity for the MIS department to offer a better service to the other departments and thereby improve its image.

The move towards decentralization means that there cannot always be operators near the computer hardware. At sites with distributed processing in different buildings it is not possible for operators to get to the distributed processor quickly enough to offer anyone reasonable service. The use of automation software removes the need for the operators to be present.

Technological Pressure

With the number of tasks that operators are required to carry out in a day it comes as no surprise that, on occasions, mistakes are made. With the number of software packages that operators have to be familiar with, it should not be surprising that well qualified operators are not always available.

In a modern computer room there are lots of software packages that operators need to be familiar with. They need to know how MVS works. They must understand the concept of address spaces. They need to know which version of MVS they are using—SP (System Product), XA (eXtended Architecture), or ESA (Enterprise Systems Architecture). And they need to know the appropriate operator commands. They also need to know how JES2 (Job Entry Subsystem 2) or JES3 (Job Entry Subsystem 3) works (preferably JES2 because JES3 is being phased out by IBM). They need to know the JES commands. They will also need to understand how any major subsystems work and the commands that control those subsystems, such as CICS master terminal commands or IMS (Information Management System) commands.

Operators also need to know how to use TSO (Time Sharing Option), ISPF (Interactive System Productivity Facility), and if its a JES2 site SDSF (System Display and Search Facility). Operators must also know how the network is built and what VTAM commands are available to control the network. There are also system monitors, such as Omegamon with their own commands which can be used to display system performance as well as modify it. Also, each of the software components produces its own form of message to the operator. At multiplatform (i.e., more than one operating system in use, such as MVS, AIX, and VMS) sites, operators need to know the command formats for each operating system

Working with all these different systems can lead to mistakes. Many sites feel that a layer of software should be introduced to integrate these various software packages and simplify system control. This is also seen as a way of minimizing the damage that can be done by an operator to the system.

On modern mainframes there are more MIPS (million instructions per second), more application programs, more messages, and more frequent calls to the operator than ever before. Automated systems operations is thought by many people to be needed to ensure a suitable level of service from the computer department, without even considering reducing operator numbers.

One of the things that can cause problems is the huge volume of messages produced by MVS and its various subsystems. Messages are continually scrolling up the console, and the majority of them can be ignored by the operator without causing any problems. However, if the operator misses an important message, a problem can occur.

Another related problem is caused by the proliferation of consoles. With an MVS console, a VM console, a TSO terminal, a CICS master terminal, an SNA (systems network architecture) console, or an Omegamon console, for example, it can be quite easy to miss a vital message. When the operator notices a problem, he or she may have to scan a number of different screens to find the cause of the problem before steps can be taken to cure it.

Operators during the day, and more frequently at the start of an evening shift, may be given a list of jobs to be run overnight. This schedule will contain the job name, the start time, and any dependencies on other jobs. Problems may occur with jobs being run in the wrong order, jobs being started at the wrong time (either too early or too late), or jobs not being started at all.

Properly trained operators can be in short supply. It may be that an installation has enough highly skilled operators to work successfully under normal circumstances, but absences due to holidays, illness, bad weather, or vehicle failure, or a combination of all four can lead to problems with staffing levels occurring. If staffers do not know the correct procedure to follow when a job fails or an outage occurs, there can be long delays before appropriate recovery action is taken, while staffers are phoned or written procedures are located.

IPLing the processor used to be a frequent event. Indeed, it sometimes took place many times a day! However, as the reliability of both the software and the hardware has improved, IPLs have become infrequent. Sometimes the period between IPLs can be in excess of six months. This means that the operators on shift may be unsure of the current IPL procedures, and the procedure may not be performed correctly, with obvious disastrous consequences. The same problem can occur when sub-systems are started.

A great many sites are aware of the problems caused by operators being unfamiliar with infrequently occurring events, and have written very full operator procedure guides. Unfortunately, in a number of sites that I have visited, it is not unknown for part of this documentation to be out of date. This may be caused by no one being responsible for it, or it may be due to the fact that a change is made in one procedure, and the relevant documentation is updated. However, dependent procedures are not altered, usually because the dependencies are not realized.

Another problem is that the documentation becomes very large, and the required item often cannot be found quickly enough. A third problem that I have come across is that the sheets of paper that are most frequently used become dog-eared, covered in coffee stains, written on, and eventually fall out of the file altogether.

At sites where the number of operators on shift are kept small, it may often be the case that the operators are busy all day servicing the needs of the computer, rather than having time to plan and control the machine. It is the operators who are controlled.

With the increased performance and complexity of mainframes, there can be too much happening too quickly, so mainframes can become virtually inoperable. IBM has estimated that 40 percent of downtime is due to operator errors. This is probably due to poor training as well as the excess of messages.

The problem is compounded by the growing use of local and wide area networks, which depend on the mainframe and its associated applications programs for their support and efficient operation. Because the scope, speed, and ability to transfer data over the network is expanding, so also are the demands on the network.

As a direct result of end user acceptance and familiarity with computers, their demand for faster and better performance has increased. This has consequently increased pressure on everyone, and increased the workload on the processor.

Cultural Pressure

The main cultural pressure causing an MIS department to move to automated systems operations is that there are fewer people to operate mainframes. The reasons for this are:

- Demographic changes mean that there are fewer young people to take the job of operator.

- The role of the operator requires greater skill than ever before; this reduces the number of people who could do the job.

- Many of today's young people in the developed world don't want to work shifts.

- Many of today's young people don't want to work for large companies.

- As older operators move into other areas of MIS, the number of existing operators is reduced.

Chapter

4

The Benefits of Automated Systems Operations

In addition to the pressures on a company to move to automated systems operations, a number of benefits can be gained. These benefits can be expressed in a number of ways:

- *Financial savings.*
  - —Fewer staff/no overtime to pay.
  - —Sites can be run unattended.
  - —Return on hardware and software costs can be maximized because they can be used to the maximum all the time.
  - —Cost savings because improved reliability means fewer reruns, outages, etc.
- *Greater availability:*
  - —Performance of extra work.
  - —More time available to perform work.
  - —Greater capacity to perform work.
  - —Improved productivity.
  - —Fewer mistakes, reduced downtime, and faster recovery mean more processor time available for end users.
- *Improved utilization:* Hardware and software can be used all the time, not just when operators or other staff are available.
- *Improved service:*
  - —Consistent service.
  - —High-quality service.
  - —Improved reliability.

—Improved speed of recovery.

—Increased accuracy.

—Elimination of human intervention and errors.

—Prompt response to critical console messages.

—Response based on expertise of best operator.

—Standardized response to problems.

—Simplified interpretation of messages—enhanced presentation for operators.

■ *Better staff motivation:*

—Elimination of manual, repetitive work.

—Improved quality of life for operators; normal working hours; no more boring repetitive jobs.

—Improved working environment.

■ *Increased security.*

■ *Increased flexibility/control of the system:*

—More controlled/less chaotic working environment.

—Can adjust quickly to changing business needs.

■ *Improved efficiency:*

—Ability to monitor several machines from a single terminal.

—Automatic recovery from application or subsystem abend.

—Less downtime.

—Duplicated data removed.

■ *Better management of resources:*

—Hardware, software, and people used most effectively.

■ *Improved productivity of end users:*

—Increased knowledge level of nontechnical staff.

Financial Savings

To make financial savings, costs must be reduced. However, a prerequisite of low cost is the achievement of high quality.

In many companies, activities are justified purely on an accounting basis. The "bottom line" is what counts. Automated systems operations can be considered in purely financial terms. The benefits in this case are:

■ Fewer operations staff required; therefore fewer salaries to pay. In a lights-out environment, no staff salaries are required.

■ Service can be offered by the MIS department for more hours of the day. This costs the MIS department nothing, but allows more time to be spent on revenue-generating activities using the computer.

- Rented software and hardware are in use for more of the period that they are being paid for. This means that the rentals per hour used decreases.

If staff numbers are to be reduced, savings can be made by the fact that new staff will not have to be employed, and the potential fees that employment agencies would have to be paid are saved.

By projecting forward current costs, it can be assumed that hardware will decrease in price (e.g., price per MIPS), and people costs will increase. By moving costs into hardware, future increases will be smaller than otherwise.

On the downside, it must be remembered that the automation software will cost money, and it will also cost money to train people to use it.

Greater Availability

Because the work previously carried out by operators is automated, it is possible to perform the activities during periods when operators would not have previously been available. This means that complex job dependencies or high-priority work, can be carried out overnight or on weekends without the requirement for human operator intervention.

Also, if some operators are retained, the automation frees them to perform nonroutine, or low-priority work, which prior to automation they would not have had the time to carry out. This means that more service is available from the computer department.

By removing a lot of the operator's interaction with the system, there will be fewer operator errors. The reduction in the number of errors means that there is likely to be fewer system and subsystem outages.

Improved Utilization

The move to automated systems operations means that system resources can be fully utilized (i.e., 24 hours per day, 7 days per week). If work at a site typically has to stop because the operators are going off shift and do not restart until tomorrow morning, automated systems operations allows work to be carried out by the processor without the manual intervention of operators.

Improved Service

Delays can occur between a problem happening in the system and the operator making the appropriate response. The introduction of automated systems operations means that the preprogrammed correct response is always carried out straightaway. It means that all activities take place at machine speed, which is much faster than the older method in which many activities had to take place at human speed. In the event of a system crash, the system is automatically brought up in the correct sequence, ensuring the minimum of disruption to users.

The net effect is an improvement in the reliability of the service. The service offered to end users becomes consistent—no more problems with some shifts performing badly—and is always high quality, always at the level of the best operator.

Improvements should be shown to end users in terms of results, as well as improved levels in service level agreements, where service level agreements exist.

Other service improvements include increased accuracy. Because there is no operator activity, there are no operator errors, and there will be a consequent improvement in service. Also, all time-related activities will start at exactly the right time. For example, jobs that have to start at 6:00 A.M. will be started at exactly that time. There is no likelihood of the operators forgetting to do it if it is performed by the software.

There are also improvements in response. For example, any messages sent from subsystems to the console will be dealt with quickly and appropriately. The response to each condition will always be the same correct response, and will always occur at machine speed rather than at human speed.

Where operators are still used—and this is at all sites moving towards automated systems operations—messages that are presented to the operator need to be restricted to important ones, and clear in what they are reporting. Automation software can offer this benefit.

Staff Motivation

At almost every site, a few operators are highly skilled and highly motivated to learn as much about computers and the company as possible. The move to automated systems operations is an opportunity to improve the skill levels of all operations staff and thereby to motivate them to do a better job. The initial introduction of automated systems operations software should free the operators from the more basic routine work that they have to perform. Some sites have found it politic to make the introduction of automated systems operations an operations department project. Although this may sound like turkeys voting for an early Christmas, it has been found to be a sensible and successful strategy. The expertise that previously had been restricted to a few operators can be used to ensure that the software performs optimally, and the extra time available to the other operators can be used by them to find out more about how things work or perform other MIS-related tasks.

The move to automated systems operations can allow operators, and to an extent database administrators and systems programmers, a better quality of life because they no longer have to work shifts; they can work more social hours, such as "9 to 5." For operators, a number of tedious, dull, and repetitive jobs are removed, again improving their quality of life. Because the staffers are no longer running around trying to satisfy the demands of the processor, they are more in control of their lives and this makes their working environment better.

The staff has the opportunity to acquire and develop new skills. On the plus side this makes them more valuable to the company. On the minus side, it also makes them more valuable on the open market. However, even that is not all bad because the move to automated systems operations usually means a reduction in the number of people required by the operations department. Losses to other companies could make any required staff level reduction fairly painless.

Increased Security

Probably the greatest threat to security at an installation is from the people working there, more than by any outsider. By reducing the number of people who directly influence the flow of work through the machine, the likelihood of corruption of data or unauthorized access to data is reduced.

Increased Flexibility/Control of the System

Too often in the past operators have been satisfying the requirements of the processor (i.e., loading tapes, putting paper in the printer, etc.); they have not been managing the processor. The introduction of automated systems operations allows them more time to take control. It also means that the service offered is greater and more flexible.

As business needs change, this increased flexibility means that workload changes can occur immediately to cater to the changed business needs.

Improved Efficiency

The efficiency of the data processing department can be improved by the introduction of automated systems operations. Efficiency improvements can be achieved in areas such as:

- The ability to monitor a number of systems and subsystems from a single console.
- Automatic and speedy recovery from application, subsystem, or system downtime.

- Removal of duplicated data in databases.
- Automatic prioritization of system faults.

In addition, all activities take place at machine speed, which is faster than human speed.

Better Management of Resources

The introduction of automated systems operations means that resources can be better managed. Equipment and staff costs can be rationalized, and staff can be used to the best effect for the success of their company.

End User Benefits

Benefits for the end users can be thought of in terms of reliability, availability, and serviceability (RAS).

The end user community are the people who use the MIS department services to help their company succeed. Benefits for the end users means that the company as a whole is benefiting, and there will be jobs for people in the future.

If the services provided by the MIS department are available for longer periods, the end users can choose when they want certain work to be done and are not faced with constraints placed on them by MIS. Therefore, they do their work at the time that is best for them and therefore best for the company. The other benefit of automated systems operations to the end user is that downtime is reduced. End users are typically not concerned with which part of the system has failed; to them it is all down. Therefore, improved reliability means that the system is up and running quicker and they can get more of their work done in a given time or do more work in the same time.

Conclusion

In the business community decisions are usually made by how they look on the balance sheet; costs and benefits have to be weighed against each other to see what is the best choice to make. From this simplistic point of view, the arguments for automated systems operations outweigh those against it.

Figures that are often quoted suggest that, as result of automated systems operations at a site, 40 percent more system can be supported by 20 percent fewer staff. In this case, system is measured by DASD (direct access storage device) cylinders, transactions, or MIPS.

Some sites have not reduced their staffing levels at all, but simply used automated systems operations as a way of improving the service offered by the MIS department and benefiting from the consequent improvement in business efficiency.

5

The Cost of Automated Systems Operations

As with all new ideas there is an associated price. Moving to automated systems operations has associated costs that might at first put people off the idea. However, it is usually the case that the outgoings are more than compensated for by the cash savings that occur later and the improvements in service. The financial outgoings can be divided into:

- Initial expenditure.
- Running costs.
- Hidden outgoings.

Initial Expenditure

Typically moving to automated systems operations involves the purchase or rental of a software package. A full list of automated systems operations software packages and suppliers can be found in Appendix B.

It is also a good idea to train some staff to use the package. These staffers will probably have to be sent away on a training course. As well as the expense of the training course, other likely costs are travel expenses, accommodation, meals, etc. It may also be necessary to pay overtime to other people covering for the ones sent on the training course.

There will additionally be a cost resulting from the amount of time that staff spend in meetings. These meetings will be initially to discuss whether to adopt the automated systems operations approach, then what criteria to apply when choosing a package. Next, time will be spent meeting the various suppliers. Time will also be spent in meetings while all those who will be affected by the policy are informed/consulted. Both time and CPU (central processor unit) resources will probably be used in testing and evaluating the likely software package before a final choice is made.

There may also be hardware costs if, for example, the automation involves the purchase of an extra screen or of a PC (or PS/2).

Running Costs

The running costs for automated systems operations involves more than the monthly rental charges which may have to be paid for the software. There is the time spent in meetings discussing how successful, or otherwise, the implementation of automated systems operations has been. Staffers who would be performing other duties will be involved writing procedures for each step in the automation. Everyone involved with the software will have to be trained in its use.

There is almost invariably a drop in productivity during the change-over period. It can sometimes take up to a year for things to be working as well after the change as they did before it—a year spent working very hard to get back to where you were before. This period of reduced productivity will have a negative impact on the efficiency of the company as a whole, and may make an impact on the balance sheet.

One cost that is sometimes overlooked is that the automated software is running on a CPU. If the execution element of the processor is carrying out instructions from the automated systems operations software, it cannot be doing other work, which it would have been if the software were not installed. It has been estimated that there is a decrease of up to 5 percent in the performance of the processor due to the presence of the automated systems operations software.

Hidden Outgoings

The previous two sections give the factors that are known to impact on the cost of implementing automated systems operations. However, others are not obvious, and they can have an unspecifiable impact.

The first factor that can impact on the success and cost of automating operations is the Luddite response. Like the Luddites of the nineteenth century who opposed the introduction of machinery because it would put them out of a job, some operators may feel that the introduction of automated systems operation software is going to put them out of a job, and they do their best to prevent its introduction. If the future of the individual operators is assured, and they are made to feel an important part of the team responsible for the introduction of automated systems operations (which they are), they will work for its success. If they do not feel part of the team, it is impossible to calculate the cost to a company.

Another factor that is hard to evaluate is the cost of the software. If the software package selected has been on the market for a long time and is known to be in use at a number of sites, it may not contain some of the latest facilities. It may therefore not do as good a job as a more recently introduced software package, and in this way cost the company money. The hidden cost of a "new" software package is that all the facilities may not have been thoroughly tested under all circumstances. This means that it may contain bugs. The site installing the software will bear the cost of being effectively a beta test site. Even if the software is not buggy, when new software is installed there is unlikely to be any other sites nearby using it that could be used to gain hints and tips from. So there is the extra cost of learning how to use it most efficiently.

6

Automated Systems Operations Implementation Difficulties

Before any activity is carried out at any installation, in terms of automated systems operations, it is necessary to consider the obstacles that will prevent this activity from taking place successfully. With automated systems operations, the biggest obstacle is probably people. This aspect is looked at in more detail in Chap. 7, "Overcoming People Problems." The other difficulties that may have to be overcome are:

- Old applications.
- Old or inadequate hardware.
- Tape-related activities.
- Responding to console messages.
- Printing.
- Job submission and scheduling.
- Recovery and restart.
- System/performance monitoring.
- Controlling the network.
- Storage management.
- Security.
- Paying for automated systems operation.

These difficulties are described below, and potential solutions are offered.

Old Applications

One problem that many sites do not at first consider is that some of the application programs in use were probably originally written back in the 1960s. The old-time application programmers probably assumed that operators would be available to perform certain activities vital to the success of the application. The applications are also likely to send lots of messages to operators. These messages need to be suppressed as part of a site's automated systems operations strategy. In fact, the introduction of automated systems operations is usually a good opportunity to update many of these old systems. Although this activity is time consuming, it is likely that the programs have been modified many times over the years and are unlikely to be efficient. Time spent now rewriting them will be paid for by fewer resources being requested when the programs are run in the future.

This is also a good time to ask the question, "Is your application really necessary?" Many sites have found that legacy applications can be combined or phased out altogether if other programs are slightly modified. The move to automated systems operations offers a site the opportunity to reduce the number of application programs that are run and to optimize the performance of the applications used.

Old or Inadequate Hardware

In the recent past, figures of 95 percent availability for the system were considered to be good. However, nowadays this figure is thought by many to be short of the mark, and a figure in the region of 99 percent is the norm. The automation audit that should accompany the introduction of automated systems operations (see Chap. 24) offers a site an opportunity to identify failing or unreliable hardware and replace it. The introduction of automated systems operations may also be a time when new hardware has to be purchased to satisfy the needs of the automated systems operations software, such as PCs. Although new hardware will cost money, this money could be recouped later by the improved efficiency of the system.

Tape-Related Activities

In the traditional computer room, operators are required to load tapes that contain application programs or data. They have to load tapes to store data produced by an application. They load back-up tapes to back-up applications, files, or complete disk packs. They load back-up tapes to restore files that may have been corrupted or deleted. They load log tapes for applications such as CICS, and they may load tapes for files that DFHSM thinks are unlikely to be used and can be migrated to that particular storage medium. Operators have to know when to put a ring in a tape. They also have to carry the tape from the tape library and put it back when it is no longer required.

Tape-related activity is the one that most sites find hardest to automate. The introduction of automatic loaders is a small step in the right direction. However, operators still need to put the tapes in the loader, and put them away in the tape library afterwards.

For fully unattended operations, it is necessary to do away with tapes entirely. Unfortunately, many older back-ups and archives will be on tape. Therefore, at least one tape drive will have to be retained at a site in order to restore these older files should it ever become necessary.

If all tape-related activity is eliminated, extra disk space must be installed. The new disks can be used to take back-ups of the files on the original disks or to mirror any changes made to the original files.

This is discussed more fully in Chap. 9.

Responding to Console Messages

An MVS operator's console is a continuously changing heaving mass of messages. Messages that are suffixed with the letter I are information messages. The majority of these are completely ignored by operators. They rarely tell operators anything that they need to know to do their jobs successfully. Other messages are suffixed A, which means that the operator has to perform an action. Operators usually respond to these, and it is these that keep operators running around working. It is the volume of these that prevent operators from controlling the system, and mean that the system controls them. Other messages are suffixed D, meaning that a decision must be made, or E, where an eventual decision must be made.

In addition to messages from MVS, there are messages from all the subsystems.

One of the first steps that many sites take towards automated systems operations is the suppression of the majority of console messages.

An additional problem with consoles is that there can be so many of them. For example, there may be an MVS console, a VTAM console, a NetView console, a CICS master terminal, etc. Operators need to know which console to look at, and may miss an important piece of information because they are looking at the "wrong" screen.

The problem for operators can be made worse in a situation when the console traffic from a remote site is also sent to the local console. There can be more messages appearing on the screen than the operator can handle.

Problems with console messages and ways to overcome the problems are discussed in more detail in Chap. 10.

Printing

For, at least, the last ten years people have been describing the coming of the paperless office. It hasn't happened, nor in the foreseeable future is it likely to! Therefore, users are going to want printed output.

No matter how automated the MIS department becomes, someone somewhere is going to have to load paper (including special stationery) in a printer. Someone is also going to have to take paper off the back of the printer and split it, and distribute it. And someone is going to be needed to sort out printer jams.

Ways to overcome difficulties with printing are discussed in full in Chap. 11.

Job Submission and Scheduling

In the old days, job submission was accomplished by the operators by putting a deck of cards through the card reader. In more recent times, jobs are submitted from TSO by end users. The jobs may be held, and it is the operator's responsibility to allow the jobs to start at the appropriate time, perhaps at a particular time of day, or perhaps when a previous job that it depends on has been completed.

The automation of scheduling is discussed in more detail in Chap. 12.

Recovery and Restart

Whenever there is a problem with software, whether it be a batch job, or something as complex as CICS, steps have to be taken to recover from the situation or, if it is unrecoverable, to restart the job or the subsystem. Highly trained and skilled operators will identify the problem quickly, and they immediately follow the appropriate procedure to get everything up and running as it should be. However, because not all operators are that well trained, there can often be delays before recovery action is taken, and, sometimes, the recovery action can be inappropriate, leading to a worsening of the original situation. Automated systems operations software or scheduler software can ensure that appropriate action is taken immediately, and that the situation is corrected.

An additional way of overcoming problems with failing applications is to write application systems that have recovery routines built into them that will start automatically.

Recovery and restart is discussed in more detail in Chap. 14.

System Monitoring

At many sites it is the operator's responsibility to watch the console and monitor the system. Operators are meant to ensure that everything is functioning correctly, and that any system problems are identified quickly, and dealt with immediately and correctly. They must ensure that all production systems are working and available to users.

Almost all sites have taken the first steps towards automated systems operations by installing monitor software. Indeed, the January 1991 issue of *The IBEX Bulletin** found that out of a sample of 910 sites worldwide, 679 (75 percent) reported at least one monitor, 216 reported two, 103 three, 39 four, and one five monitors.

More details about automation and monitors are given in Chap. 16.

Controlling the Network

In the past, networks have been notoriously error prone. Not only has there been a variety of software in use, but also there have been hardware problems including the local PTT (Post, Telegraph, and Telephone company). The introduction of VTAM, rather than BTAM (basic telecommunications access method) was considered by many to be a great leap forward.

With the continued growth of the network for transaction-based systems, such as CICS, it became even more important to ensure network availability, and to identify and correct any errors as they occurred.

Indeed, once a potential problem is identified, it may be necessary to initiate additional tests to discover the extent and scope of the problem.

With VTAM and NetView, it is possible to automatically restart network resources, and automate many other aspects that previously required network operators.

Problems with automating network control are discussed more fully in Chaps. 17 through 19.

Storage Management

Until recently, the only storage management available at an MVS site was defining group names for disks and restricting users to putting their files on those disks. It was typically an operations support job to police files to ensure that they were placed on the right disks. As disks became full, it was again an operations support job to start a COMPAKT or DEFRAG job to place all the files at one end of the disk and leave the free space at the other.

The introduction of SMS (IBM's System Managed Storage) addressed the areas of data integrity, residency, performance, and access. As a direct consequence, fewer work-hours need to be spent performing administration/management activities on files because more of the process is automated, and clearly more will be in the future.

The IBEX Bulletin is a monthly survey of IBM mainframe and compatible sites throughout the world. It is published by Xephon plc.

SMS is available as DFSMS (Data Facility Storage Management Subsystem). DFSMS is not itself a product, but an agglomeration of RACF (Resource Access Control Facility, an access control package), DFDSS (Data Facility DataSet Services, a back-up/restore package), DFHSM (Data Facility Hierarchical Storage Manager, a file migration package), DFSORT (a sort package), and DFP [Data Facility Product, a VTOC (Volume Table of Contents) and VSAM (Virtual Storage Access Method) catalog utility package]. New with DFSMS/MVS Version 1.1 are DFSMSrmm (Removable Media Manager) and DFDSM (Data Facility Distributed Storage Manager).

SMS should monitor and control the placement of data across all DASD. It should control back-up cycles and schedule appropriate recoveries. It is meant to go a long way towards overcoming the problems associated with storage management.

SMS and other related storage management issues are discussed more fully in Chap. 21.

Security

In the past the operators have in many ways been responsible for security. They may not have set up the entries in SYS1.UADS, but they would have been expected to notice any security violation messages as they appeared on the console screen, and would have taken any appropriate action.

Security can be automated by the use of RACF (now part of DFSMS). It is responsible for controlling access and reporting violations. Other network software can perform additional security checks.

Operators were also in the computer room and would query any outsiders about their presence. If the computer room is a lights-out area, there is no one to see intruders. This means that additional physical security is required to prevent unauthorized access to hardware.

If sites wish to install hand scanners, retina scanners, and the like, these can be linked to an automate systems operations program which would permit certain actions, and take appropriate action in the event of attempted security violations.

Problems relating to security and automated systems operations are discussed more fully in Chap. 26.

Paying for Automated Systems Operations

The cost of automated systems operations may be hard to justify initially because it will require extra expenditure. However, this initial cost is usually more than compensated for by the savings that can be made over time.

The financial outgoings associated with automated systems operations are described in Chap. 5.

7

Overcoming People Problems

A number of problems have to be overcome before automated systems operations can be introduced, but perhaps the biggest problem is people. These same people are also the biggest asset that a company has. People often appear to be remarkably conservative, preferring to do things the way they know, rather than changing to a way that may be better.

With the introduction of automated systems operations, resistance can come from operators and from other related departments, such as data entry. People fear that they may be agreeing to the introduction of something that will take away their jobs and leave them unemployed. They also fear that they will have little chance of further employment because all the other companies with MIS departments will be automating and will be getting rid of their operations staff.

It is also not unknown for management to be resistant to the introduction of automated systems operations. Managers who measure their "empire" in terms of the number of people who report to them will feel threatened as this number is drastically reduced. They are the first people who need to be convinced that automation is for the good of the company. Senior management need to be convinced of the importance of automated systems operations to the success of the company in order to supply the necessary funding.

Figure 7.1 is meant to illustrate, as a cartoon, peoples' perception of automated systems operations and show how these perceptions are different for different groups of people and how they do not fit together. Once management is convinced of the need for automated systems operations, they must ensure that everyone is working together to achieve the same things and sharethe same perspective.

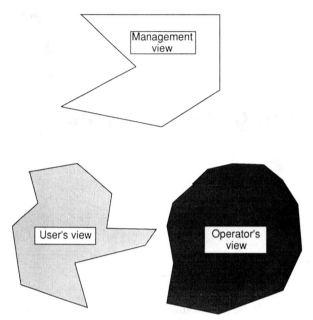

Figure 7.1. People's view of automated systems operations. Managers must modify people's views so that everyone is working towards the same goal.

Management Perspective

When implementing such a major change in the working environment, management is usually recommended to follow a number of steps to successfully implement the changes:

- Create a picture of what the future system could look like. All people who are to be affected by the change should be involved at this stage and should be invited to contribute to this vision of an ideal environment.

- Clearly identify the benefits that will come from the automation. The benefits for the individuals affected and also the benefits for the company must be clearly stated for everyone to see.

- Decide what resistance there will be to the proposed changes and decide on the best method of dealing with it.

- Plan the project and carry it out.

- Ensure that, after each stage in the change to automated systems operations is introduced, follow-up activities are performed to reinforce in peoples' minds the benefit of the changes so far and to set the scene for further changes.

Reasons for Resisting Change

Some of the reasons that people give for resisting change are summarized below:

> There is no need to change.
> I'll lose my job/area of expertise.
> I won't know what to do when it's all different.
> Better the devil you know, that's what I say.

It is important for management to be aware of peoples' feelings in this matter and take appropriate steps to ensure that all people involved with the change to automated systems operations have a positive attitude towards it.

When people concerned feel that there is no need for change, it is a good idea to hold meetings with them and pass on the information that will show them why the change is to their advantage. In addition to meetings, it is necessary to keep the people informed about what is going on and encourage them to adopt the same view towards the change as that held by management.

Where people fear the loss of their job or their area of expertise, it is important to stress the benefits of the change, and the opportunities for the future that it offers them. It must also be emphasized that they will not lose their job as soon as the change is complete. Managers must ensure that there is a complete retraining program available for the people affected, and these people must be encouraged to take part in it.

Where people are conservative and do not wish for any changes to take place at all, management must again take the time to explain to these people the opportunities that the proposed change offers to them. They must also ensure that the people are aware of the training programs that are to be offered to them, and they must be made to realize how the change will benefit the company and ultimately benefit them.

Strategies for Success

Staff need to be educated so that they can see the benefits to themselves of an automated systems operations policy. Data center staff must appreciate the change that will occur in their role. It will change from one of machine supervision to one of user support.

Staff must be made to realize why the change must happen. They must also realize that they will not lose their livelihood.

In order for it to succeed, all involved personnel must be part of the project. The affected staff are needed to implement and oversee the physical aspects of automated systems operations implementation.

A large commitment to training must be made from the outset. Staff need to be assessed and retrained to make the best use of the skills they have.

Wherever possible, management should attempt to break down the barriers that have grown up between staff departments affected by the automation. Departments involved would include operations, technical support, DBA (database administrator), information center, etc. The staff must realize that the aim of automation is to make the company more successful, and this success can be achieved by people working together for the good of the company. Staff would learn about the problems experienced in the other departments. In some circumstances it may be possible to swap people between departments.

Everyone must realize how much the company will benefit from the change.

End users will regain some of the sovereignty that they lost when their departments were first computerized. They will benefit from better service, although they will probably have to do more work after the automated systems operations implementation. End users must be educated so that they see the advantages offered.

Management must believe that automated systems operations is possible, and will increase the competitive advantage of the company.

Operators must see this as an opportunity. Operators may regard the introduction of automated systems operations as threatening. They seem to be losing their jobs and having their career path redefined. They need to be educated to see the opportunity for personal and career development that automated systems operations offers them. In fact, a career progression path for operators and other affected staff must be published.

The idea of automated systems operations should be introduced at group meetings. The advantages to the company and to the people involved should be emphasized. Managers must be prepared to spend a lot of time communicating with people. It is important to ensure that all people involved are aware of the steps being taken and the time frame, and some people may require counseling and support if they think that their job will disappear in a month's time. Managers introducing the automation must ensure that staff, senior management, and end users are on their side. Staff must be made aware of the provision for retraining, and managers must ensure that retraining courses are suitable and beneficial.

If a lot of resistance is met, managers should increase the amount of communication—more meetings, posters, newsletters, and group discussions.

A word of warning: Tread carefully when dealing with unions. In this case it may be necessary to invite people who do not work for the company along to meetings to show them how the project will work. They must see that the union members jobs are not at risk because of the automation, and more jobs may become available when the company becomes more successful in the market. Unions may also have to agree to new job descriptions for their members, and this may involve two or more unions agreeing to changes in practice.

Measurements of performance must be made before the implementation and afterwards so that the benefits of the automation can be seen. Managers must ensure that all staff are made aware of the success of each stage of the project.

In a situation where a company feels that it may still have too many people, the numbers can be reduced by natural wastage, retirement, attrition, and a policy of little or no recruitment. This is a fairly painless way of reducing the head count. If staff numbers need to be kept up at any time during the migration to automated systems operations, subcontracted staff can be used on short-term contracts.

8

How to Implement Automated Systems Operations

The exact procedure to be adopted at a site in order to implement auto-mated systems operations will depend on any number of factors. This chapter sets out to utilize the experiences of a number of sites that have carried out the automation procedure and to describe the areas that need to be taken into consideration, and the general steps that need to be followed.

Almost every site that has gone through the automation procedure has said that, if automated systems operations is the destination, this is not the best place to start from. This is because no site ever thinks that it is in a good initial position to go through the automation procedure. The reason is that any steps towards the automation that have taken place in the past have always been as a response to some situation or event. They have rarely been as a result of detailed planning, and invariably without thought for the future. A necessary consequence of this is that each piece of software, such as a scheduler and monitor, may be doing a satisfactory job, but may not be able to be integrated with each other.

To carry out the implementation of automated systems operations, the following steps should be taken:

- Define the objectives.
- Ensure management support.
- Form a project team.
- Review current processing.
- Review current hardware and software.
- Define installation policy.

- Plan the implementation.
- Specify clear and achievable targets.
- Implement the automation.

Define the Objectives

Different sites have differing ideas about what they mean by automated systems operations. Different people at the same installation may have different ideas about what is meant by automated systems operations. Therefore, it is important that everyone involved in the project should be working towards the same goal. Whether the goal is a reduction in console messages, unattended operations, or full automation of every aspect of the system, it is important that everyone is aware of the target they are aiming for.

It is usual to set short-term objectives, followed by long-term objectives. In this way, a full picture can be kept in mind when working on the smaller details. The project should be arranged so that an early, successful result is achievable (usually console message management). This success gives everyone confidence in the project.

Also, as objectives are achieved, the success should be publicized. This means that measurements will have to be taken before and after the implementation so that the success can be shown statistically.

Ensure Management Support

When the MIS department have made up their mind that automated systems operations is the way forward to offer a better service to other departments in the company, they must then ensure that senior management within the company are going to support the project. The company's business plan must include the automation of systems operations, and all those taking part in the project must know that they have the full backing of the management. The senior managers are the people who will have to agree to the budget proposals to pay for automated systems operations.

Many sites like a mission statement to be produced. This mission statement must briefly define the scope of the project. This statement can define project objectives and responsibilities. If a mission statement is produced, it is important to avoid certain pitfalls. For example, a political speech should be avoided—something that is all puff or hype, but lacking in any real substance. It is also important to keep it within achievable limits. Overambitious statements can put too much strain on the development team such that they fall well short of the proposed target. The third pitfall is one of language. Care must be taken that the statement is not ambiguous in any way. However, if the legal department is called in to remove all ambiguity, care must be taken that the statement is still comprehensible to members of the public.

Forming a Project Team

Once it has been decided what is to be achieved by automated operations, and that everyone in the company is behind the project, it is necessary to form a project team that will carry out the automation. In almost all cases, the project will to a large extent involve the automation of operations, and the project will be most successfully carried out if operators are heavily involved in it from the beginning.

The project team should contain the following job responsibilities:

- Project manager.
- Project leader.
- Technical analysts.

The project team should be made up from everyone who is going to be affected by the automation, especially operators. It should also be led by someone with experience of leading a project. Other staffers who could be represented in the project team are:

- Systems programmers.
- Network people.
- Application representatives.
- End user manager/representatives.
- System development analysts.

The project team should also be able to co-opt other staff onto the team for short periods when those staff have expertise or knowledge required for the success of the project. The project team must have people in it with experience in selecting software and dealing with vendors.

During the automated operations part of the project, around 10 percent of operators should be taken off day-to-day work to work on the project and plan automation for the future.

The project team should develop a comprehensive set of terms of reference. They should examine in detail the current roles of every member of the MIS department, and see how each person's role interacts with every other member of the department. This can be built up into a map showing the logical relationship between people and the level of integration that is necessary for the success of the project.

Review Current Processing

A large number of projects involve system or application changes where too little thought or time was spent finding out the state of play before the introduction of the new software/hardware or whatever. To ensure that the automated operation covers all areas currently covered by human operations, a review of current processing must be performed. Included in this should be an event questionnaire to find which events currently involve human intervention. This information can be used later to reduce the level of human involvement.

Some of the areas that need to be considered include:

- Service windows and associated costs.
- Any problems associated with the provision of a service.
- What human resources are required.
- Planned applications—what changes need to be made to them to fit with automation.
- Current performance levels of the operations group.

Review Current Hardware and Software

As mentioned in the previous section, it is important to know exactly where you are starting from. It is important to know what hardware is currently in use so that any alterations can be clearly identified. The same is true with software.

Achieving automated systems operations may require modifications to some or all of the following:

- Hardware.
- Security—both physical and security software.
- Environmental monitors.
- Application programs—they must assume no external intervention.
- Processing control facilities—allowing batch and on-line work to proceed without operators.
- Manual functions—these must be eliminated or automated.

Hardware

Once the current hardware is known, any special hardware requirements of the automation software packages that are to be introduced can be assessed. It will then be possible to see if the hardware requirements can be met from current hardware, or whether the purchase of additional hardware is needed. For example, it may be necessary to purchase a new PC. Other hardware requirements may be automated tape loaders, on-line laser printers, and graphic terminals. It may also be a useful time to replace older hardware.

The review of hardware may also be looked on as a useful time to consolidate such things as maintenance contracts with suppliers.

The main hardware that needs to be reviewed is clearly the processor itself. It is important to establish that the processing power can handle the new demands that will be placed on it by running the automated operations software and later the automated systems operations software. It must also be sufficient to handle the extra workload that will be placed upon it after the operations department is automated and additional service is available to end users.

Environmental monitors may need to be linked to the automation software. If conditions in the computer room become too wet/dry/hot/humid/ etc., there may not be any humans about to notice this. Therefore, environmental sensors should be linked into the automation software so that the automation software's escalation procedures can be used to alert a human that there is a problem. If possible, the automation software should perform the recovery activity. Therefore, new sensors may have to be purchased (heat/smoke, etc.), and these will have to be linked to the automation software.

New pagers may have to be purchased to facilitate automatic call-out of staff.

Software

It is necessary to find out what mainframe, midrange, and PC software packages exist at a site. Information that should accompany the package name in any list produced includes:

- Which processor range it runs on (mainframe, PC, etc.).
- Number of copies.
- Number of licenses.
- Version, release, and modification level.
- Purchased or leased.
- When purchased/rental per month.

This information can be used to ascertain whether all the software is used and which packages could be dispensed with. It can also be used to ensure that the levels are compatible and whether newer releases should be purchased. It is also worth checking that the software packages will work with whichever new software is to be purchased. Again any necessary upgrades should be purchased.

The check also offers the opportunity to identify any unauthorized or pirated software that might be in use. Subsequently, licenses can be applied for or users can be restricted to using the company-designated software.

This checking procedure also gives an opportunity to find out where the documentation for the software is. Many entrenched MISers feel that real men don't read documentation. However, to get the most out of a product it is always a good idea if someone reads through it, no matter how badly written it might be. It may be possible to have some documentation on-line so that users can look up information whenever they need to. The project may be used as a good time to do this.

Define Installation Policy

There is no point in each member of the project team thinking that certain things should and should not be done. From the beginning, an installation's policy should be clearly laid out. This policy should include information such as:

- What information is to be included in Info/Man or similar information-disseminating software.

- What are the escalation procedures in the event of a problem that cannot be handled by the automation software.

- Should stand-alone dumps be taken, or should a re-IPL start straight-away after a system failure.

When new application programs are written as part of the automation project, it is necessary to ensure that:

- The way programs are written is standardized.
- Program layouts are standardized.
- All in-line comments are standardized.
- All updates are standardized.

Plan the Implementation

The planning stage also involves certain business decisions being made, and it is at this stage that the biggest mistakes may be conceived. Aspects of the planning stage that must be performed are:

- Identify all requirements.
- Decide product evaluation criteria.

- Consider all solutions.
- Produce costs, benefits, and risk analysis reports.
- Plan for recovery.
- Testing and maintenance.

Some of the decisions that have to made include:

- Should the number of suppliers be minimized?
- Does the role of the operations department need to be redefined?
- What level of operator involvement is required?
- What can/should be automated?

Identify all requirements

A decision has been made that automated operations is the first step towards a solution to a problem that the company has been facing, or a way of helping the company become more competitive. At the planning stage it is necessary to identify all the requirements of the automated operations solution for that site. It is no good being well into the project and deciding that another criterion needs to be satisfied. If unattended operations is the goal, then all aspects of that for the particular site must be considered at this stage.

Decide product evaluation criteria

If a software package is to be purchased, it must be decided what hurdles the software has to clear. Suggested questions that a site might ask are given in Appendix A. Each site will weight the answers differently when choosing its software.

The software selected for the automation should offer certain facilities. These include:

- *Reversal of the usual way console messages are used:* Automation of console management involves moving from people watching consoles to ALERTS appearing on screens. The screen should remain completely empty except when a problem occurs. Then an alert message should be sent and alarms may sound. The software may not also automatically page an operator.

- *Simplification of operator interfaces:* When using multiple subsystems and/or multiple platforms, the operator needs to know numerous different command formats to perform the same activity, such as stop a subsystem. The automation software should allow a software front end to be built (e.g., under ISPF) that allows the operator to specify the action required and the system to be actioned, and leave it to the software to build the actual command for that subsystem.

- *A single control language should be used across the automation.*
- *The software, should be modular in nature:* If one part fails, the rest will continue to work.
- *The software should allow dial-in:* It should be usable by remote operators.

More details of software requirements for each type of automation can be found in later chapters. Appendix A contains a list of questions that can be asked when selecting automated systems operations software packages.

Consider all solutions

Surprisingly, very few sites ever consider all the solutions to the problem that they are faced with. A colleague of mine recommended brainstorming sessions. In this everyone associated with the project sits round in a room and suggests anything that they think at the time might solve the problem. All suggestions are recorded and no evaluation of a suggestion is made at the time. It is only after the session that all ideas are evaluated. At one site, an idea that was followed up was to move to a facilities management contract instead of automated systems operations. Without taking care to avoid it, a typical site will sit down, come up with one idea, and everything else will be geared to fit that first idea whether it is the best or not.

Produce costs, benefits, and risk analysis reports

The production of costs, benefits, and risk analysis reports is very nearly standard for most projects. If there is more than one possible course of action in the implementation of automated operations, it is imperative that reports are produced for each solution. Although this may take time, it should result in the best solution being adopted.

Plan for recovery

Throughout the implementation of automation, thought must be given to what will happen if part of the automation procedure fails, or if all the automation software fails. For example, if the automation software fails to start all the IMS regions, there must be a fall-back procedure so that the remaining operators know exactly what to do to manually start all the IMS regions. Also, if any part of the automation fails to perform its task, it must inform people immediately. It is not satisfactory to discover that the automation software has failed to perform a particular task hours after the task should have been performed. If the whole automation software fails, a recovery plan must be in place to allow MIS service to still be offered to end users.

Contingency planning is also an issue here. Thought must be given to how to implement automated systems that will operate correctly during contingency mode operation. An automated operations system should be designed so that it is not adversely affected when it runs on different hardware or when additional workloads are migrated onto the system. Also thought must be given to how the automation system can facilitate the process of going into contingency mode.

Testing and maintenance

Testing of the automation software like any other new software is important. Problems can occur with automated systems operations when multiple pieces of software are linked together. Sometimes a minor change to one automated system will have an unanticipated effect under a particular set of circumstances. For example, two different automation products might interact destructively when they react to the same message.

Another reason why testing is important is that many sites have automation software using MVS, JES, SMF, and program product exits. The use of exits can create a programming and maintenance nightmare, especially during upgrades. One advantage offered by automation packages is that they can replace exits with vendor-supplied software. For example, SMS can replace the MVS IGGPRE exit in allocation.

Should the number of suppliers be minimized?

Many sites have a preference for "one-stop shopping." This means that they prefer to get the bulk of their software from one or two companies. In many instances these two companies are IBM (because it supplied the operating system) and Computer Associates (because it has taken over lots of the other companies that used to supply software). There are generally fewer compatibility problems if software is supplied from a single source.

Some installations prefer to shop around for software because they say it offers them greater freedom of choice. However, even they will acknowledge the difficulties that this policy sometimes causes in terms of support when products do not work properly together.

Does the role of the operations department need to be redefined?

The operations group will be expected to fulfill certain objectives. The introduction of automated operations can modify those objectives. Changes may have to be made in areas such as:

- Security.
- Scheduling.
- Funding.

Security. As automated operations is introduced, new security problems must be dealt with. The questions needing an answer are:

- Who is allowed to use the automated systems operations tool?
- Who is allowed to change operational procedures?
- Who is allowed to start and stop the automated systems operations tasks?

It is also worth thinking about what would happen if the automated systems operations tool ceased to function at any time. Who would know what to do, especially if the tool could not be restarted. Some sites have relied on exoperators working in other departments to come back to their old jobs and run the system. The drawbacks to this are that in five years' time there may not be enough of those exoperators to do the job, they may have forgotten much of what they knew, and the system may have changed out of all recognition (e.g., an operating system migration from VSE to MVS).

Scheduling. Two aspects to scheduling need to be considered. It is necessary to schedule the introduction of automated operations. It is also necessary to alter regular schedules to allow for testing of the automated operations procedures, and when they are implemented, nightly schedules can probably be speeded up because checks and dependent job releasing will be speeded up.

Funding. The whole point of the automated operations procedure is for the company as a whole to be more competitive. In order to make money, it is going to have to spend money. One thing that the planners need to do is evaluate what new items need to have money spent on them. However, they must ensure that the cost of the planning stage to the company is not too high.

Costs will include:

- Software (purchase or rental).
- Implementation effort (possibly including weekend overtime payments, and processor time taken away from production work).
- Maintenance costs (usually per annum).

See Chap. 5 for more details.

Benefits of automation will also have to be pointed out to management, operators, systems programmers, end users, and other affected staff. These benefits may include:

- Reduced staff salary payroll (if fewer operators are required, or less overtime payments are required).
- Reduced hardware costs (if file placement on DASD is automated, fewer new DASD will be required.
- Improved level of service and performance.

See Chap. 4 for more details. Senior management must be confident that automated systems operations is good for the company so that they allow enough of the budget on automated systems operations to ensure its success.

What level of operator involvement is required?

Experience shows that operators should be involved from very early on in the project. They should not only be consulted, but should make up a large part of the project team. It is considered by many that the whole thing should be an operations department project. In this way, the knowledge of the operators can be used, and their motivation for the project is positive.

What can/should be automated?

As discussed in Chap. 3, usually business reasons have prompted a site to adopt a policy of automated operations. There are usually areas that are demanding some kind of automation. At the planning stage, it is best to start with the easier things and then move to the harder ones. The usual first stage is some kind of reduction in console traffic.

The aim is to eliminate everything that does not have to be done. The working premise is that operators should do nothing. When something comes along that must be done, it becomes a candidate for automation. It is always worth double-checking whether something can be eliminated. If something is so complex that it cannot be automated, it must, in the early stage of the automation, be left to the operators to operate.

Figure 8.1 shows what can happen if current procedures are automated rather than adopting new and improved procedures.

Specify Clear and Achievable Targets

When implementing the project, it is a good idea to specify the final target and to specify smaller targets on the way. The targets should be associated with deadline dates, and they should be realistic in terms of what can be

Current procedures

A mess

Automated procedures

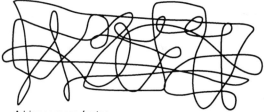

A bigger mess faster

Figure 8.1 Rethink procedures before automating.

achieved in a given time. The first law of project management states that whatever the time allowed for a project, it will take at least one third longer to complete, even allowing for this law.

When setting up the automated operations project, it is not enough to simply automate operator's procedures. If this is what happens, in two years' time, when the automation of operations is complete, the procedures in use will all be two years out of date. The project team must consider the way that the data center could be run in, say, five years' time and make that the automation goal.

The speed at which the implementation takes place depends very much on the access a site has to other sites that have undergone similar implementations. This is because the usual starting level of expertise and experience is around zero, and access to experienced people and to their procedures can speed things up considerably.

It must be clearly stated for each target, what is to be achieved, by whom, the deadline for its achievement, and at what cost.

The team implementing automated operations need to know:

- Manual operations procedures.
- Priorities.
- Schedules.
- Management objectives.
- Agreed service levels.

At the outset it will be necessary to find out what automation software products are available, and evaluate them to see which is the best for the particular installation.

Once the product is selected, it must be installed and customized. People must be trained to use it, and it must be tested rigorously. The impact of the product on the rest of the operation's procedures must also be reviewed.

Implementing Automated Systems Operations

Once all the planning decisions have been made, and the project team is set up, the following procedures can be adopted.

- Areas of human intervention must be identified.
- What is necessary to eliminate those areas must be decided.
- The necessary changes must be incorporated into all new software, and existing software must be changed accordingly.
- The simplest changes must be implemented first.
- All other changes can subsequently be implemented.

Human intervention

The manual functions at a site should be identified so that these functions can be eliminated. These manual functions should include those performed by people in roles peripheral to operations, such as tape librarians, data entry, and the like.

The manual functions at a site usually include some or all of the following:

- Console interaction, such as answering WTO messages.
- Selecting, loading, unloading, and replacing tapes or cartridges.
- Data entry.
- Printing and its distribution.
- Scheduling work.
- Restarting failed jobs.
- Checking batch totals.
- Monitoring the system and subsystems.
- Restarting failed systems and subsystems.
- Network operations.

Eliminating human intervention

When automating, it is useful to assume that operators should do nothing and plan accordingly. The following is list of some of the ways that can be used to reduce or eliminate human intervention.

- Automate all operations activities.

- Eliminate all procedural steps that do not add value to the data entered into the computer. People between data entry and report arrival do not add anything. They cost money, and may slow things down.

- Let end users view the MIS department as a self-service area. Allow users to enter data (where this cannot be collected directly), schedule processing, and distribute output. In this way, users will appear to control the flow of their job from the comfort of their terminals.

- Eliminate bureaucracy wherever possible. People signing for reports or giving permission for jobs to be run, or other old-fashioned bureaucracy should be eliminated. All processing on a job that is to be done should be controlled by the end users from terminals. Therefore, the bureaucracy is unnecessary.

Some practical ways of achieving this are:

- *Automate console responses.* This area is discussed fully in Chap. 10.

- *Adopt a policy of reducing tape usage, and eventually eliminating it altogether.* Details of ways of reducing tape usage are described in Chap. 9.

- *Eliminate data entry by people.* If data has to be entered into the computer, wherever possible it should not be entered by data entry clerks, but by point of creation apparatus [e.g., electronic cash tills, POS (point of sales), ATM (automatic teller machine), or whatever other data collection devices are available]. Data transcribed from one piece of paper to another, keyed in (perhaps twice for verification), and other human intervention causes delays and can introduce errors. All new applications must be written to allow for the collection of this data. It should be remembered that, in this situation, the applications need to be available 24 hours a day.

- *Eliminate printing and its distribution.* Details of how to reduce the amount of printing carried out by the operations department are discussed in Chap. 11.

- *Reduce manual intervention in batch jobs.* Details about scheduling and automated restart/reruns can be found in Chaps. 12 and 14.

- *Automate system monitoring.* More details are in Chap. 16.

- *Perform storage management activities.* Automate the administrator's role in ensuring that files are placed on the correct disk, and that disk space is used optimally while ensuring optimum performance. Also ensuring that files are backed up regularly, and that data duplication is reduced or eliminated. The need for human activity in this area can be reduced or eliminated. For more details, see Chaps. 20 and 21.

- *Eliminate the need for technical specialists wherever possible.* The technical expertise should be in the software rather than in the heads of people.

Automation Stages

The following is a summary of the stages that a site usually goes through when carrying out automated systems operations.

Stage 1

The first step usually involves message suppression. It is usually fairly simple to achieve and the benefits are immediately apparent. The operator's life becomes simpler.

The next step is to automate simple operator replies to messages and introduce any other software that the operator can use easily and that makes life easier.

Stage 2

Stage 2 involves message flow integration and subsystem management. Many more messages can be answered automatically and subsystems can be started up and shut down automatically. A problem management system can be introduced for messages and problems that the software cannot deal with.

The next substage is to reduce printing and use a print management system, and introduce a job scheduling package.

This stage should also see the integration of the automation products, including monitor software.

These steps allow a movement away from standing in front of consoles to being able to work from PCs located elsewhere.

Stage 3

This sees the automation system able to correct most errors that occur.

Once all the operator-related activities have been automated, it is possible to move on to coordinate multiple MVS platforms. And from there to automate other platforms, such as VM and VSE, or to move to non-IBM platforms, such as DEC or Hewlett-Packard, etc.

Systems programmer-type activities and data administrator activities can be automated, including dynamic load balancing across multiple platforms, and dynamic system tuning and configuration management.

9

Automated Systems Operations and Hardware

Many people remember what it was like to be a "real" operator.

A real operator:

- Knew how to make a 4-inch loop for the printer so that special stationery could be printed.
- Knew which way round to feed in paper tape.
- Could take cards from the card punch and put them into the hopper of the card reader the right way round without dropping them.
- Could carry two removal disks, one in each hand with arms out stretched.
- Could power on and off the hardware.
- Could IML and IPL without using a manual.
- Could fool a tape drive into thinking a tape had a ring in it.
- Could start batch jobs, check totals on output, load special stationery into the printer the right way round, clear printer jams, sort output, deliver output to end users.
- Could use a plotter.
- Could burst, decollate, and edge trim four-part stationery with three sheets of carbon.

Tell that to a modern operator and they won't believe you.

The modern operator doesn't do all the things that a "real" operator had to do because so much has been automated already. No one sends data to a paper tape printer, which then has to be loaded in. The data is sent directly to the computer. The paper tape printer and reader are consigned to the dustbin of history. Modern printers do not have physical loops in them that throw the paper forward. The new printers allow this process to be controlled by software.

It is probably only VM sites that talk about cards these days because they use virtual readers and punches. The old card punches and card readers are rusting away at a dump because data can be entered directly from a terminal, or other input device, such as a bar code reader, and they are no longer needed.

Removable disks are hardly ever used. Fixed disks now have many times the capacity of the removables, so there is no need to use them. Advances in hardware have made the operator action of changing disks obsolete.

The increased reliability of all hardware means that the old quick fix of powering it off and then on again is rarely necessary. The processor so rarely crashes that operators hardly ever see an IPL, let alone an IML.

With the introduction of scheduler software and other enhancements (see Chaps. 12 and 13), operators do not have to control the flow of batch jobs or check totals of jobs before the next one can start.

Operators are still involved with printing and loading tapes. Chapter 11 looks at ways of automating printing. This chapter looks at ways of automating tapes.

Tapes

It is not uncommon at busy mainframe sites for the operators to be loading hundreds of tapes per day. These would include back-up tapes, DFH migration tapes, archive tapes, off-site back-up tapes, father/son generation tapes, data tapes, and many others. The tapes could be selected from a tape library with thousands of tapes in it. Operators have to know when to put a ring in a tape. They also have to carry the tape from the tape library and put it back when it is no longer required. Tape usage is labor intensive and error prone.

In addition to numerous 3420 reel-to-reel tapes, many sites have the newer 3480 cartridge tapes. Tape-related activity is the one that most sites find hardest to automate.

Some sites have found it advantageous during the introduction of automated systems operations to migrate to 3480s. As well as having to buy lots of new cartridge tapes, it is important to check all JCL to ensure that it specifies 3480s rather than 3420s. It is also necessary to transfer all data to the new tape media. This includes all archive tapes including those stored off site or in fire safes and which rarely ever see the light of day.

Some estimates have suggested that up to 50 percent of operational problems are associated with tapes. Certainly the need for a tape can be the reason for a job waiting and taking longer to complete than similar jobs that do not require a tape.

Automation options

A number of options are available to a site to reduce the amount of tape activity or to eliminate tape activity all together.

Reduce usage. Tape usage can be reduced by the introduction of a tape management system, such as CA-1 or TLMSII. This reduces the work associated with tape handling, and may improve the quality of retention procedures.

IBM's offering is the Removable Media Manager (RMM) component of DFSMS/MVS Version 1.1. This software, in association with a 3495 tape library dataserver, ensures that the cartridges in use at a site are fully used rather than only partly used. This makes much better use of unused tape capacity and reduces the number of tapes required. IBM describes its product as offering tape library and inventory control and tracking.

IBM introduced IDRC (Improved Data Recording Capability) on 3480s. IDRC compresses data, and offers an 80 percent reduction in tape requirements, thus reducing tape usage. It also offers faster data transfer rates, which helps with SMS dataset placement problems.

Another way of reducing tape usage is to back up changed data only, rather than perform full pack back-ups.

Tape dataset stacking utilities can be used to reduce the number of tapes used and thereby reduce the amount of tape handling by operators.

Tape handling can be automated. This can be achieved by using a tape stacker or an automatic tape loader. The introduction of automatic loaders is a small step towards automation. However, operators still need to put the tapes in the loader, and put them away in the tape library afterwards.

While not actually reducing tape handling directly, the use of bar code scanning and PC to mainframe communication can reduce the amount of work carried by people in managing a tape library and keeping track of back-up and off-site tapes.

Eliminate usage. An Automated Tape Library (ATL) can be used. An ATL stores 3480 cartridge tapes in a central repository and interfaces with system resident tape management software. When the system requests a tape mount, the ATL uses a robotic arm to retrieve the correct volume and mount it. Tape mount requests are satisfied much faster than if an operator is involved. Examples of ATLs are StorageTek 4480 Automated Cartridge System (ACS), Memorex Telex 5400, Automated Tape Library (ATL), and Comparex 6388 Automated Cartridge Library (ACL). The 4480 has a capacity of 6000 cartridges. The 5400 has a capacity of 658-5152 cartridges. The advantages of using such a device are:

- Few manual tape mounts are required.
- Very little operator time is spent loading tapes.

- Less time is spent performing back-ups that rely heavily on tapes.
- Back-ups can be performed when operators are not on site.

IBM announced the 3495 tape library dataserver on May 19, 1992. This is an ATL based on their 3490 magnetic tape subsystem. The product, which can run from 44 feet to 92 feet in length, consists of an enclosed structure along which the robotics run. Using ESCON channels, the device can be located up to 14 miles from the processor. It can store up to 45TB of data. It is controlled by the Removable Media Manager component of DFSMS/MVS Version 1.1.

Tape usage can be reduced if old applications are rewritten so as not to use tapes. Likewise, new applications must be written that do not use tapes.

An alternative to the use of tapes is a mass storage system. Examples, from Masstor, include the Masstor M960, which stores 110GB of data, and the M1000, which stores 1.2TB.

Another alternative to the use of tapes is RAID (redundant arrays of inexpensive disks) technology. This is a disk drive that contains a large number of small platters and heads. Performance is meant to be enhanced because the platters spin faster and the heads have to travel only small distances.

A third alternative to tape is the use of an optical storage subsystem, such as the DW 34800 from the Data/Ware Development Corporation. This can store between 190GB and 760GB of data. It is a write-once, read-many (WORM), which is fine as a replacement for tapes because many tapes are used for exactly that use.

The traditional replacement for tapes is extra disk space. The new disks must be purchased and can be used to take back-ups of the files on the original disks, or to mirror any changes made to the original files. To save disk space, this back-up data can be compressed.

Problems with back-ups. With the growth of 24-hour processing, the back-up window has been reduced to such an extent that there is not enough time to carry out the necessary tape back-ups. Incremental back-ups only are possible.

Recovery becomes very difficult because of the large amount of data backed up and the fragmentary nature of the back-up because modified or new files only are backed up and the period since the last full pack back-up is a long one. The DFHSM ABARS (aggregate back-up and recovery software) offers some help with this (see Chap. 20 for more details).

In addition to files stored on the mainframe, there is a need to back up PC files and perform recovery for PCs and file servers. This is possible since the introduction of SystemView-based workstation products [e.g., NVDM (NetView distribution manager)], and means that end users do not have to run their own data centers. It simplifies the lot of the end user.

The solution to the problem of almost useless tape back-ups is to mirror data to disk in real time, preferably at a remote complex. Some functionality for this is available now from Andor, and CNTI offer CHANNELink which allows locally attached DASD to be physically located at a remote site. This not only provides a back-up of the data, but also offers a back-up site in the event of the main site experiencing a catastrophe.

Mainframes

Improvements in the performance of mainframes have reduced the amount of operator involvement. In the near future, system failures can be reduced by using hardware enhancements announced by IBM. These include:

- *Fault tolerant dynamic memory arrays*, available on selected water-cooled ES/9000s. These processors contain enhanced system fault tolerance through the use of spare logic array chips that become active should the main chips fail. Data is moved from failing chips to the new chips without system or application interruption.

- *Concurrent channel maintenance feature*, available on some water-cooled ES/9000s. This allows a failing channel to be repaired or replaced without interrupting the processor's overall operation.

- *Processor availability facility*, available on the air-cooled frame models and water-cooled models of the ES/9000. It makes recovery from most processor failures, in multiprocessor environments, transparent to the user.

- *Subsystem storage protection*, available on selected ES/9000 models. Subsystem storage protection enables the isolation of application software failures, reducing the frequency, scope, and duration of CICS outages. CICS downtime caused by application storage violation is expected to be reduced by up to 50 percent with CICS/ESA Version 3. This product provides a greater level of application isolation by exploiting the Subsystem Storage Protection feature.

- *Extended recovery facility (XRF)*. XRF automation for CICS-DB2 (DataBase 2) environments offers automatic detection and fast recovery from system failures. Since recovery is automated, failures are masked from the end user and do not require operator intervention.

Other hardware features

A number of other recently introduced hardware features make the mainframe more reliable and therefore reduce the need for operator involvement.

The ES/9000 Sysplex timer can be used to synchronize CPUs even if there is no Sysplex present. This facility could be used as a useful time-stamping mechanism for audit trails and for transaction recovery on high-throughput systems. Amdahl has offered a similar clock facility for some time for very high throughput applications, such as airline booking systems.

Fiber optic cables associated with ESCON (Enterprise System CONnectivity) allow dynamic reconfiguration (hot plugging). Fiber eliminates the electrical spike that is inevitable in connecting and particularly in disconnecting copper.

Because the use of ESCON allows control units to be situated at a great distance from the mainframe, it is possible, for example, for all DASD to be located in their own lights-out area. Because this lights-out area would be unattended, it would be necessary to monitor the air conditioning, humidity control, and temperature. IBM has announced ESCON Monitor to do this. The ESCON Monitor System (ESCMS) can be used at unattended data centers. It uses a hardware monitor and sensor adapters to allow remote hardware to be controlled from a central site. ESCON Monitor allows remote devices to be monitored from the mainframe or it can communicate with an automated systems operations product. ESCON Monitor communicates with ESCON Monitor Sensor Adapters, which attach to devices. The adapters can power on/power off the remote devices.

A PS/2, running as an ESCON Analyser attached to an ESCON Director, can be used to monitor errors on fiber optic channels.

Also MVS/ESA Version 4.1 allows a resysgen operation without shutting down. MVS 4.2 can activate the new configuration without shutting down and needs ESCON for microcode loading.

Until recently, IBM has considered the resident operating system (software envelope) and mainframe serial number (hardware envelope) to be inextricably linked and consistent. However, performance enhancements will be available in the future, when hardware and software envelopes bear no direct relationship to one another. A Sysplex will enable a task to be carried out on the most suitable processor within a tightly or loosely coupled CEC (central electronic complex). This means that, within a CEC, unloaded CPUs will actively demand work. Because a Sysplex can control a mixture of processors from any part of the ES/9000 range, it may be impossible to tell which processor is executing a particular piece of code.

Reasons for Using a PC in ASO

Many sites start introducing automated systems operations without considering the use of PCs or PS/2s. While PCs are not a prerequisite of automated systems operations, they do offer a number of useful facilities. PCs perform three main roles:

- Doing things that MVS-based automated systems operations packages cannot, such as IML or IPL.

- Doing things that mainframes do not do well, like getting VTAM to dial out and page someone's beeper.

- Helping MVS, for example, ensuring that the TOD clock is set properly.

PCs can also perform standard automation activities—intercepting messages and issuing commands—and PC-based automation systems consume no mainframe CPU cycles. On the downside, the mainframe has to do more work because it has to solicit information from the PC through command/response dialogues.

In the past, IBM's micro-to-mainframe products have primarily focused on providing terminal emulation capability to its users. IBM introduced an APPC/PC product for the MS-DOS environment that provides an LU6.2/APPC capability. However, the memory available for MS-DOS applications was severely restricted.

The introductions of OS/2 EE has provided a suitable platform for APPC/LU6.2 communication. Currently, PC-to-mainframe connections are based on PU2.0 nodes, which limit their connection to host initiated mainframe applications. An upgrade to PU2.1 is required to provide peer-to-peer connectivity. This would allow any PU2.1 node to initiate a conversation with another PU2.1 node and eliminate the need for a mainframe as part of the network or conversation.

There are three main areas in which the PC can offer more than the mainframe:

- Consolidation.

- Global view.

- Graphic user interface.

The PC can handle traffic from various subsystems, such as VTAM and IMS, and allow the operator to hot key from one sort of session to another. The software can act as the operator for these diverse services as the situation demands.

The other big advantage offered by PCs is that they are much better at presenting information, particularly color graphics. In the event of a disaster at the computer site, flood, fire, earthquake, and the like, the PC could be used to switch work to the disaster recovery site. The PC can then be used to monitor and control the automation software at this standby site, and end users can continue working as if nothing had happened.

An example of PC-based product is AutoMate/XC from Legent, which runs under OS/2 and Presentation Manager, and provides a graphic operator workstation for external systems automation of IBM, DEC, and Tandem environments, as well as any system accessible through asynchronous communication.

10

Automated Systems Operations and the Console

Automating activities associated with the console is usually the first step towards automated systems operations that a site takes. It is an area in which success can be achieved fairly quickly and simply, and it is an area in which success can not only be demonstrated statistically, but it is apparent even to the untrained eye.

The types of activities associated with console automation include:

- Message management.
- Automating responses.
- Time-dependent operator activities.
- Event-driven operator activities.
- Other.

In the early stages, operators should be able to look at the console and see clearly what needs doing. They should not have to wade through lots of irrelevant or arcane messages. The ultimate aim of console automation is to remove the requirement for operators altogether. The software would perform all time-dependent activities. It would also check that devices, etc. were on-line, and take remedial action wherever necessary. All information messages would be suppressed, and those that required responses would be answered automatically and correctly. Where the software was unable to choose the correct response, the message would be sent to the user who initiated the job that caused the message to occur (the user should know what response to give), or an operator would be paged to dial in and answer the message, or someone performing another role that included an operator would receive the message on their screen.

For most sites, this ultimate aim is a long way off. The usual first step is to reduce the volume of messages reaching the console to those that require an operator response and, where possible, make the wording of the messages more comprehensible.

The console automation system must work with all subsystems—CICS, IMS, VTAM, etc.

One of the main reasons for automating console activities is to reduce the number of operator errors. The type of operator errors that occur include:

- Mistyped commands.
- Misread message—operators making an inappropriate response.
- Misinterpreted message—operators making an inappropriate response.
- Inappropriate action by the operator, causing major problems because of system complexity.

This kind of operator error can be reduced by:

- Creating a consistent message interface.
- Reducing the volume of messages.
- Raising the skill level of the operators.

Benefits

The benefits that result from automating console activities include:

- Service is improved.
- Routine messages are responded to correctly.
- No messages are forgotten or ignored.
- Time is saved in responding to messages because the correct response does not have to be looked up in a manual.
- Console responses come at machine speed, not at human speed, and are therefore much faster.
- Down time is reduced because responses to messages during restarts (and re-IPLs) are faster and accurate.
- Time-dependent routine operator functions are performed automatically on time.
- Money can be saved by reducing the number of operators required.

Error Avoidance

Adopting even a simple automated operations system can reduce the amount of data being presented to operators, and therefore improve their response to the important information. If the automation reduces the more humdrum tasks that operators have to perform, it will reduce the likelihood of error. Automation is a way of reducing the amount of work that operators have to do and therefore reducing the number of mistakes that they could potentially make. Also, as operators have fewer messages to attend to, they should respond quickly and accurately to the few that they do have to deal with.

The operator's console can control the whole MVS/JES system, and an erroneous keystroke can cause havoc. The use of some automation software can prevent the more catastrophic disasters.

An example is the JES2 drain command, $P. This will drain all JES2 activity, prevent any new activity, and is usually used before shutdown. However, it is not unknown for this command to be inadvertently entered. It is also difficult to diagnose what the problem is when it has occurred. Automation can be used to send a message to the operator asking him or her to confirm any severe command like this.

A similar example occurs with the JES2 block cancel command, $CJnnnn-mmmm. This cancels jobs in the range nnnn to mmmm. It is useful if a group of jobs need to be deleted, and saves the operator keying in all the job numbers. If, in error, the operator puts the higher number first, followed by the lower one, all jobs in the system and all print files will be deleted except those with numbers between the two numbers specified. This is quite the opposite of the intended command. An automation system can prevent the use of this command, or send a message asking the operator to confirm the enormity of the cancellation required.

Message Management

One factor that makes operations more complex than ever before is the increasing volume of messages sent from an increasing number of applications and subsystems. With the increase in the processing power of modern computers, applications and subsystems deliver the same number of messages as before, but do so faster. Average message rates of 10 messages per second are not uncommon, and peak arrival rates of 100 per second have been recorded.

The increase in the number, type, and arrival rate of messages means that they become impossible to digest, correlate, or act on. One solution tried at many sites is to split the messages up and send certain types of messages to certain consoles. In this way, for example, tape load messages are all sent to the operators who only load tapes. This solution, while reducing the amount of message traffic on the main console does not solve the problem of the number of messages being sent, nor does it automate the process of dealing with messages. The solution is to reduce the number of messages that appear on the console.

Ideally, the operator's console would remain blank until something is wrong with the system, in which case a meaningful message should appear on the screen. This complete reversal of the way that console traffic currently works cannot be achieved straightaway. It is usual to go through stages of suppression.

Traditionally a console full of messages is telling the operator that lots of things are working. Message suppression reverses the idea by making an empty screen mean that everything is working perfectly.

Before any automation takes place, operators have to filter out the unimportant messages from the important ones when looking at the screen. Good message suppression software will do this for them.

When deciding which messages should be suppressed, operators should be fully consulted because they have the most experience in this area. An estimated 60 to 80 percent of messages at a site are information messages.

If a policy of message suppression is adopted, it is a good idea to ensure that new application programs do not send any messages. It is also useful if older applications are looked at to see if the messages they send can be suppressed.

Each MVS message contains an action code. The action codes are shown in Fig. 10.1.

In addition to messages from MVS, the message suppression activity must work on all the other subsystems—JES, CICS, IMS, VTAM, etc. Figure 10.2 illustrates message flow in MVS. MVS contains MPF (message processing facility), which allows certain messages to be suppressed. To be truly successful, it is, perhaps, a better approach to use a rule-based system.

As a first stage in message suppression it is necessary to:

- Collect message traffic to the console.
- Collect message traffic from other interfaces.
- Analyze the message traffic.

Action code	Meaning
A	Action required
B	Decision required
E	Eventual action
I	Information only
W	Wait - processing is stopped until action is determined and performed

Figure 10.1 Action codes and their meanings.

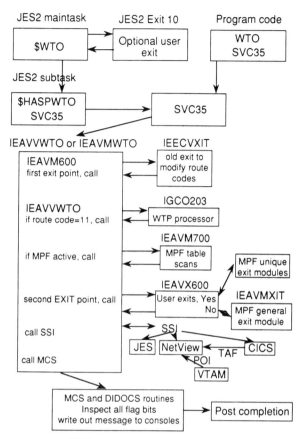

Figure 10.2.   MVS message flow.

The traffic should be analyzed by:

- Message frequency.
- Message id.
- Time distribution.

This information can be used to select the messages that should be suppressed at source. It also clearly shows the most frequent messages. If software is not available to do this, it can be done by analysis of the SYSLOG using an in-house program or, for example, the SAS system (from the SAS Institute).

If all else fails, it is possible to get from IBM, on Info/MVS, a list of messages that can be suppressed with little impact on the system.

Although messages are not displayed on the console, it is important that they still appear on SYSLOG. This is so that full auditability is maintained. It also helps when tracking down a problem.

One problem that can occur with simplistic message suppression is that suppression of a single "unimportant" message is a "good thing," but if that same message is being sent to the console 100 times a minute, clearly a problem is occurring that needs resolving. However, the operator will be totally unaware of it. Simple suppression will not allow the recognition of frequent arrival rates of a message, and any problem that could be identified in this way is left undetected.

Message Processing Facility

The MVS Message Processing Facility (MPF) is limited in scope in terms of access to information, flexibility, and ease of maintenance. However, its supreme advantage is that any site with MVS already has it, and it is possible for the system programmers to start using it straightaway. Its other advantage in economic terms is that it is already paid for, or it might be viewed as being free.

MPF can be used to control message display and message processing. The MPF characteristics to use are defined in PARMLIB member MPFLSTxx.

MPF can be used for message suppression, message retention (by AMRF—Automatic Message Retention Facility), passing messages to an automation system, or invoking a user exit for additional processing. However, this method is usually too simplistic, and what is required is a "suppress this message if...," or "display this message if..." type of reasoning. Again MPF can be used, but exits must be written in Assembler. MPF syntax is shown in Fig. 10.3.

If, for example, the message IST020I is issued by VTAM showing that initialization is complete, the user exit can be invoked. The user exit could be a simple start command which will call a SYS1.PROCLIB member. The PROCLIB member could contain other start commands, such as START TSO.

It is worth noting with this approach that MVS recovery automatically deactivates a failed exit. Therefore, each exit ought to be created as a separate load module. If multiple exit routines are linked together into one large module and a single routine fails, all the routines in that exit are also automatically deactivated.

MPF syntax

message-id, SUP(yes/no),RETAIN(yes/no),AUTO(yes/no/token),USEREXIT(name) comment

---

Figure 10.3. MPF syntax.

Working with MPF involves being in Supervisor state with Protect Key 0. It is not something to be undertaken lightly. Mistakes can have systemwide implications.

SubSystem Interface

Message automation tools, apart from MPF, work on the MVS messages presented to the MVS SubSystem Interface (SSI). Some will also access other interfaces, and issue commands to those interfaces. The only subsystems that can use the SSI are ones that are defined in PARMLIB member IEFSSNxx.

Each message has certain characteristics. It will have:

- Textual information.
- Usually a number.
- Color.
- Highlighting.
- Roll deletable.
- Job name.
- Job number.
- Initiator of message.
- Time and date of delivery.

The message handler needs access to the SSI. It also needs to access:

- Interface to other systems (for multi-CPU sites) over SNA sessions.
- Information from TP monitors, such as CICS or IMS.
- Information from SNA network, from PPI (program-to-program interface) and CNM (communications network management) interfaces.
- Information from performance monitors.
- Information from database management systems.
- Information from key applications.

With this information, a realistic picture of the state of the system can be built, and messages can be responded to, in the most appropriate way as a result of this information.

When installing a message handler, it can be useful to divide actions into those that can be based on the content of an individual message, and those where the action depends on further information. This division separates the simpler systems, like MPF, from other more complex ones.

Not all unsuppressed messages need to be displayed at an MVS console.

They could be routed to TSO or other on-line system consoles. This can make life easier if the operator is working from a terminal outside the machine room.

Any messages that are sent to the operator can be made clearer by color coding them by subsystem, application, or severity/priority.

Automating Responses

The messages that appear on the console requiring an operator response can be usefully divided into three categories:

- Consistent.
- Investigative.
- Complex.

One of the benefits of analyzing message traffic is that it is possible to identify what percentage of responses to messages at a site can be automated.

The benefit of this automation is that responses are consistent, fast, and correct. It means that the performance of the best operator on site is available 24 hours a day, seven days a week.

One point to bear in mind when setting up the automation system is that the format of messages from systems and subsystems may change with new releases of those systems and subsystems. The automation system must be built with enough flexibility to allow for this.

Consistent

As a result of a specific message occurring, the same response is consistently given. An example of this type of action is the response to a tape allocation recovery message. The response is always NOHOLD.

Automation of messages requiring the same response is the easiest to perform and quickly yields noticeable results. An estimated 15 to 20 percent of messages at a site are in this category.

Investigative

Sometimes replies cannot be given immediately because more information is required than is available in the message itself. An investigation is necessary to decide what action is appropriate. However, once the extra information is obtained, the decision making process is always the same—e.g., restarting a failed component such as an IMS BMP (batch message processing) region.

To automate replies to messages that require extra investigation takes longer than for straightforward responses, more coding and testing are required. The savings and benefits that can be derived depend on the amount of time and effort spent developing the system.

Complex actions

Complex actions are the ones that the operators are not sure what to do with, the ones that vary with different jobs or different circumstances (such as time of day, etc.), or the ones that require the operator to call out support to decide on the appropriate response. Responses to the message can vary. Automating these messages is very hard. Not enough information is contained in the message or available on the machine to make a decision. Nor does the same set of circumstances usually occur often enough to initially make it worthwhile telling the software to watch out for it. Fortunately, these type of actions are usually limited to around 2 to 5 percent of the total. These can be channelled through the NetView focal point processor to one of the operator consoles, if an operator console is to be retained. What to do with these messages—i.e., who to send them to—can be decided by an automated problem management system.

Because the messages requiring complex actions do not occur that frequently, a way around the problem of how to deal with them is to remove them. It may, for example, be sensible for the message to be sent to the users irrespective of whether they are on TSO, CICS, or IMS. The users would take the appropriate action because they would have enough information to make a decision. Alternatively, an operator could be paged who would dial in from a PC and answer the message. The other alternative is to install an expert system and spend a great deal of time getting all the possible information available for the expert system to make a decision.

Time-Dependent Operator Activities

At most sites, a large number of commands have to be performed at certain times of day. An example might be CICS, DB2, and IMS systems that must be started at 7:00 A.M. each day and shut down at 8:30 P.M. Address spaces must be started and shut down in the right sequence. These commands could be performed by the automation system. This can be done using NetView CLISTs.

Event-Driven Operator Activities

Operators stare at the console for long periods of time, absorbing information about what jobs are running, how many TSO users are on, etc. At first, the action is positive, but after a time (perhaps 20 minutes) information absorption becomes passive—a kind of osmosis. During this more passive stage, error messages can be missed, or lack of action on the part of, for example, a TSO user can be missed. It is possible, with automation software, to identify TSO users who have been idle for a site-determined period of time. These can be automatically abended with an S522. The benefit of doing this is that machine resources are saved, and another TSO user can get onto the system. The USERMAX = nn value is specified in SYS1.PARMLIB. This specifies the maximum number of TSO users allowed on the system. The actual value may be lower if the MAXUSER value in the IEASYSxx member is reached.

A similar situation occurs with TSO users who are stuck logging on. This seems to occur more frequently with the wider use of session managers. The automation software can perform a D TS,A command. This will give the user-id as *LOGON*. If the command is performed every 15 minutes and each list is checked against the previous list, it is possible to identify which session is stuck and to cancel it. This again frees resources.

Other event-driven activities include automatically performing recovery activities following a message indicating, for example, a terminal hang; and balancing the system workload to ensure systems thresholds are not exceeded.

Other

In addition to these facilities, advanced console automation should:

- Combine commands. In many instances, operators are required to enter very large commands, or they have to enter long sequences of commands. These can be automated, and initiated either by the automation software as a response to a particular message or by a much simpler console command.

- Bind together other automation packages.

- Perform what would have been traditionally operator-initiated events; for example, the operator may wish to check that all DASD are on line. This can be done with a CLIST. Any exceptions can be flagged to the operator.

- Allow operator commands to be issued from one console to any other mainframe platform without the operator needing to know the correct format for the command on the other platform.

Console automation can now include the attachment of PC-based programmable console software, performance product interfaces, and virtual VTAM session technology. Some PC-based platforms allow management of multiple MVS images, attachment to non-IBM systems, beeper support, and voice identification systems.

11

Automated Systems Operations and Printing

It seems that no matter how "electronic" systems get, people always need some documents or reports printed on paper. Traditionally this printing has been part of the operator's role. And in the future, no matter how automated the MIS department becomes, it looks like someone is going to have to load paper (including special stationery) in the printer. Someone is also going to have to take paper off the back of the printer, split it, and distribute it. And someone is going to be needed to sort out printer jams!

The move to automated system operations is an ideal time to take a good look at the hardware, procedures, and software in use at a site for printing. In terms of hardware, the things that need to be considered are:

- The age and quality of the hardware that is in use.
- The amount of hardware required to perform the required tasks.
- The location of the hardware.

The introduction of automated system operations also allows the procedures associated with printing to be reexamined and modified where necessary. Questions that could usefully be asked include:

- Is it necessary to print all the reports currently being printed?
- Is it necessary to keep printing within operations?
- Could printing be performed by end users/specialist printers?

Hardware

Newer printers are less likely to jam than older ones, and so an old printer that is in constant need of attention could be a prime candidate for replacement by a newer reliable one.

Newer printers can print faster than the older ones. This means that most of the printing required could be done during the period when operators are on site, if a policy of keeping operators during "9-to-5" is adopted and printing is to stay as an operator activity. It is often a high-risk activity to print out of hours. It is Murphy's law that says anything that can go wrong will go wrong—and printing will go wrong.

In purely financial terms, replacing an old failing printer can pay for itself fairly quickly in terms of the greater volume of work that can be produced, and the reduction in the amount of operator time spent nursing it. More output is produced not only because the printer prints faster, but also because it breaks down less often.

Installing pre- and postprocessing hardware can automate that part of the system and can be justified financially because it reduces people costs while improving the service. For example, there are roll feeders for use with continuous stationery printers. For postprocessing, for example, there are cut sheet feeders that can help.

Another method of reducing human involvement with printing, and also of cutting costs is to cut out the use of preprinted stationery. If this is not possible, then the use of special stationery should be reduced as much as possible. The use of AFP (advanced function printing) printers offers high enough resolution to remove the need for preprinted stationery—provided color is not a requirement.

If a cutsheet printer (such as 3828) is used, the peripheral operations jobs such as bursting, trimming, and decollating multipart stationery is no longer necessary. This is a useful move away from human involvement towards automation. However, paper trays in the printer still have to be filled by a human.

If full unattended operations is the goal for automated system operations at a site, the choices are either to give the end users a printer so that they can control their own output or to outsource the bulk printing. This would require sending a tape to, or a telephone link with, a specialist printing organization who would print the required output and bring it back for distribution in the company.

Procedures

The introduction of automation can be used as an excuse to cut out a certain amount of printing, reports in particular. If reports are not printed, and no one complains, then there is no need to print that report. This simplifies things and saves money. Therefore, the best procedure to adopt is the one that will eliminate all unnecessary printing.

If users expect to print large volumes of output overnight, and collect it first thing in the morning, the introduction of automated system operations may be a good opportunity to modify their expectations. If operations are to keep responsibility for printing, it is best if it is done during the day.

If operators are to retain responsibility for printing, the number of times that they come into contact with the printer should be reduced. This can be achieved to a degree by ensuring that only large print files come off the 3800 printer, all other print files should be printed on users' printers. Also, it is possible to use roll feeds on 3800. This gives up to six hours of unattended printing. The problem with roll feeders is that they take up a lot of space. The other problem is that the heavy paper rolls could be hazardous if not carried and stored correctly.

There is no reason why users could not have their jobs modified so that very short summary sheets were produced. These sheets could be printed first thing in the morning and be available to the user by the time the user has a cup of coffee and opened the mail.

Another option is for the print file to be written to disk. The users can then read the file from a terminal any time they want and as often as they want. It might also be an option to microfilm the file and give the user the microfilm to view. If most print files are stored on disk this can result in a large financial saving because a great deal of paper is saved.

When multiple copies of the same report are required, savings can be made if one copy of the report is produced for a user, and that user photocopies the report for the other people who require a copy.

Savings in time spent printing, and in the amount of paper used, can be achieved by consolidating one-page reports. This eliminates the front and back pages which are unwanted.

Another way that paper can be saved is if an E-mail system is installed. Rather than printing memos to be sent to different people, users can send E-mail to each other. The memos can then be read at a terminal, and a hard copy is hardly ever required.

Traditionally, control reports are produced for batch jobs by the data center. These reports need to be examined by humans to identify any problems and if necessary to recover data. To eliminate this printed output, quality control should be built into applications or separate jobs should be run that check for problems. In the event of a problem, an automated problem management system can be used to call someone. In a sophisticated set-up it could also be clever enough to offer advice on how to solve the problem.

The introduction of automation is an ideal time to look at ways of saving money. One that can cut costs more or less in half, although not particularly helpful in the automation process, is to print on both sides of the paper.

Software

In terms of automated system operations, the best solution would be to install software. The software that looks after the printing and distribution of reports is called a Report Distribution System (RDS), Print Management System, or Print Distribution Management (PDM).

If a report distribution system is installed, it can look after print files in the period following their creation by an application, up to the moment prior to their physical printing.

An RDS can run as a started task, as a batch job, or under the control of CICS. If it runs as a started task, it should be consistently available. If the RDS runs as a batch job it can work in one of two ways. Job steps can be added to capture the spooled output, or an appropriate scheduler submits a batch job to gather the output. If the RDS runs under CICS, it adds a lot of overhead to CICS. It is only worth considering this option if most printed output comes from CICS.

An RDS offers the following advantages:

- Improved quality of service to users.

- Errors in report handling are eliminated. If the reports are not handled they cannot go wrong (in theory).

- Reduced amount of paper used, if some reports not printed.

- Reduces number of printers required.

- Reduces wear and tear on printers.

- Fewer reruns caused by lost or damaged reports.

- Improved security for sensitive reports.

- Provides an audit trail for all reports.

- Users can view reports on line, be responsible for report distribution, and can arrange for the printing of exception reports.

- Users may have the ability to reformat their reports.

- Reports can be retained and archived for later use if necessary.

- Reports can be sent to local printers, to remote printers, to disk, or to tape.

- Reports can be read from TSO or from PCs.

The spool files created should be stored rather than printed. They could be stored as VSAM files or DB2 files to allow fast access to them for viewing by users. The reports should be available using a number of keys, for example report name, sysout class, job name, user, or age.

If a report distribution system is in use, it can be used to ensure that users who only want to see part of a report get that part only, and not the whole of the report. Many reports are only looked at when things go wrong, so it can be very cost effective to make not printing the report the default, and make printing it an exception.

A report distribution system should limit access to reports to authorized people only, and allow multiple access to reports by authorized people. It should also allow reports to be stored compressed or encrypted.

The RDS should be able to deal with reports that do not have a destination. These could be sent to a default file and retrieved later when the owner shows up.

Typically, the MIS department is responsible for much of the printed output at a site. They should ensure that they are in the forefront of the nonuse of hardcopy. End users will learn by example. It also saves rain forests.

Report distribution systems should be able to bundle reports for one department and send it to them. This reduces the need for multiple deliveries, and ensures that the delivery address is correct.

The RDS should be able to automatically download reports to a user's PC where this is a requirement. This allows the user to manipulate the data in the report using PC reporting tools, which are often more user friendly and save mainframe MIPS.

Figure 11.1 illustrates the way that a print management system works.

Examples of print distribution and management systems are given in Appendix B.

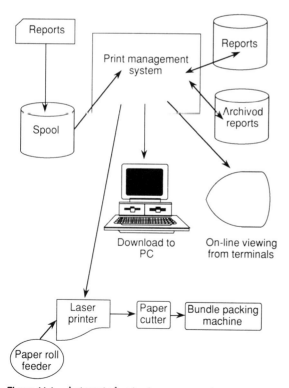

Figure 11.1. Automated output management.

Chapter

12

Automated Systems
Operations and Schedulers

In the old days, job submission was accomplished by the operators by putting a deck of cards through the card reader. In more recent times, jobs have been submitted from TSO by end users. The jobs may be held, and it is the operator's responsibility to allow the jobs to start at the appropriate time, perhaps at a particular time of day, or perhaps after a previous job that it depends on has completed.

Traditionally, one person (sometimes called the scheduler) would write down on a sheet of paper the order that jobs were to be fed into the card reader, and any totals that needed to be checked before a dependent job was fed in, or which jobs needed to complete successfully before the next one could be submitted. The operators would ensure that the jobs followed the prescribed pattern. There would necessarily be a delay between one job finishing and its dependent job starting. This set-up worked successfully at many sites over a number of years. However, where problems did occur, it was usually due to human error.

The use of cards was phased out so that problems due to the card deck being dropped and the cards being fed in the wrong order became a thing of the past. Users could submit work from their terminals. The work could be held until released by the operators.

It is also possible, using JCL, to hold a job until a particular start time is reached. It will then be released. Whether it starts processing depends, of course, on whether there are any initiator address spaces set to that class available.

JES3 and Scheduling

At many MVS sites that ran a lot of batch jobs, JES3 was installed. JES3 allows the interrelationship between a complex network of jobs to be specified. In effect, it means that all the jobs can be submitted at one time, and JES3 can be left to control the release of the jobs at the appropriate time. One more place where human error could occur is removed. The relationship between jobs is specified using the //*NET card. For example, job A may contain the card:

```
//*NET HC = 0,RL = (B,E)
```

HC refers to the hold count; in this case zero. RL refers to the jobs that can be released after the successful conclusion of this one. If the hold count is zero, the job can start straight away. When it completes successfully, jobs B and E will have their hold count decreased by one. Job E might, for example, contain the following //*NET card:

```
//*NET HC = 2,RL = F
```

This job has a hold count of two. It means that two earlier jobs must complete successfully, and those two jobs must both have a //*NET card with RL = E in it. When job E completes successfully, it will subtract one from the hold count of job F. When the hold count for a job reaches zero it will start.

Scheduler Packages

Many sites took the first steps towards automated system operations of batch work by purchasing a scheduling package to ensure that batch work was run quickly and successfully.

Schedulers are basically software packages that perform the starting of jobs at the right time and the dependency checking part of the operators job. It would be nice if software were able to determine the optimum time to run a batch job and schedule the job to run at that time.

End users should be able to schedule their own work by telling the automated scheduler what their requirements are. This is viewed by end users as an improvement in the quality of service offered to them.

An ideal system would allow parameters (e.g., date, batch number, etc.) to be passed to the job without end users knowing anything about JCL. End users should be able to query the status of their job and other jobs that are related to it where a job dependency situation exists.

Some of the benefits of an automated scheduling tool are:

- *The elimination of manual intervention.*
- *Improved quality of service:* The software ensures that jobs are not forgotten or run out of order; and that deadlines are met.
- *Time savings:* Time is saved because job set-up and schedule preparation activities are eliminated; processor time is saved because the next job in a suite of jobs is started as soon as the previous job completes.

- *Reduced operating costs:* The processor is used optimally and no jobs are waiting to be started that could be running. Because fewer reruns are necessary, cost savings can be made. Money is saved by not having to pay someone to write schedules, etc.

- *Fewer complaints:* The improved service means that the number of complaints received is reduced.

- *Less problem solving time:* The improved service also means that the amount of time spent in meetings resolving problems is reduced.

- *On-time production:* Production work is completed on time.

- *Better service levels:* Service level objectives are met.

- *Fewer errors:* Errors in job submission, job sequencing, tracking dependencies, and identifying restart/rerun situations are eliminated.

- *Balanced workloads:* Workloads can be balanced across slow and peak times, thus increasing throughput and capacity of the system.

- *Automatic housekeeping activities:* For example, datasets should be deallocated, and a failing job step determined.

Schedulers can reduce the number of operators and production control staff required. It frees them from the mundane tasks and allows them to concentrate their expertise on exception handling.

In a modern site the task of job scheduling has matured into production control and workload management. Products offer more than just the ability to submit jobs at specified times; they manage the interrelationship between jobs, datasets, hardware resources, processing errors, and system availability.

All jobs, dependencies, and interrelationships have to be defined to the scheduler. Calendars containing holiday dates and the like will have to be given. Rerun and restart considerations must be explicitly spelled out. The scheduler must know whether a job step needs to complete before a dependent job can run, or whether the whole job must complete. It must also know of negative dependencies, i.e., where two or more jobs cannot be run at the same time for whatever reason. In terms of workload management, it is useful if, for example, a job should require five tape drives, that the scheduler waits until five tape drives are available before starting the job. This prevents the job sitting in an initiator waiting for the tape drives and means that the initiator can be used by another job.

It is also a useful facility if the scheduler allows for manual override in the event of special instructions one week or in an emergency situation. Operators may need to add jobs or remove them. The scheduler should automatically start batch jobs. In a situation where tapes are going to be required by batch jobs that will actually run during an unattended period, it is useful if the required tapes can be prepared beforehand by the scheduler informing the operator which ones to get from the library and load in the tape loader. It is a useful feature if the job scheduler can also keep track of nonscheduled jobs running on the system.

Before the arrival of automation software, when a failure occurred in a job step, the job stopped. Attempts were made by the operator to fix the problem and, if this failed, others might be called out. With an automatic problem management system it is possible to call people as soon as a problem occurs. If they are at home or at a remote site, they can use remote diagnostics by dialing up from a PC, and they can fix the problem.

With a scheduler, when a job fails it should be able to select an appropriate job to start. This may back out the changes that have been made and/or restore files, and notify someone of the problem, or it may automatically restart the job at the correct point in the JCL. The recovery jobs that are to be used in the event of a batch job failing must be known to the scheduler.

In the event of a system crash, the scheduler should know what jobs were running, and perform restart/rerun activities for them. To do this the scheduler will need checkpoint datasets.

The scheduler must deal with production processing errors and schedule definition errors.

Job scheduler facilities

The following is a list of facilities offered by most scheduler packages:

- Jobs can be started based on date, time of day, completion of previous job, or other related event.
- The schedule can be dynamically modified at any time.
- End users are able to schedule their own jobs.
- On-line systems can be started and stopped; many batch jobs are run against, for example, CICS files. The CICS system needs to be stopped before the batch job runs. Once the job completes, CICS could be restarted.
- The processing workload must be balanced to optimize resource usage.
- Schedule in a multi-CPU environment.
- Restart abended jobs, and perform restore/recovery activities.
- Eliminate the need for paperwork or human intervention.
- Allows end users to submit work without knowing JCL.
- Allow end users to find the status of their batch jobs themselves.
- Check job completion.
- Have automatic event reporting.

Associated Facilities

In addition to straightforward scheduling of batch jobs, it can be useful if the scheduler can offer extra facilities, or if additional software can be used with the scheduler to provide additional and related facilities.

In terms of using the services offered by the MIS department, it is useful to keep in mind the idea that not only does the end user know nothing about how the computer works, he does not want to know how the computer works. This means that end users should be able to easily specify their requirements, sit back, and let the automation software take care of it.

Automatic JCL scanning ensures that the JCL associated with a job is correct and that the job will not abend due to a JCL error. An alternative is to let the scheduler build the necessary JCL. This removes another task from the end user, and from the MIS department.

Batch jobs sometimes abend because the correct procedure or program to use is in the wrong library (PDS-partitioned dataset). Usually because it has been updated/enhanced by a programmer. If automation (library) software is used, this will ensure that the right procedures, JCL, programs, and so on are in the right datasets whenever a new production job goes live, or when an existing one has been updated.

Something that happened more frequently in the past, but that still does occur, is job abends caused by lack of disk space. It can be useful to run software that prevents abends due to lack of available disk space. Stop-X37 from Empact Software is an example of software that will do this.

Other associated software enhancements are discussed in Chap. 13, "Automated Systems Operations and Batch Run Balancing."

13

Automated Systems Operations and Batch Run Balancing

At a typical site, there are a number of significant applications that produce batch reports. These batch reports were traditionally verified and balanced by a human, usually the operator. If there are many applications and lots of reports, this clearly ties up a lot of human resource. Using humans for this type of work can be uneconomical, operators may make mistakes, and they may cause a delay in the delivery of the reports. And yet there are still a number of sites that do this. Automation of this activity can be cost effective, increase accuracy, and may improve the speed that reports reach end users.

This kind of output checking is given different names at different sites. The most common are balancing, report verification, reconciliation, and simply checking the output.

This batch balancing activity falls into two types:

- *Commercial balancing* involves verifying values, e.g., sales amounts, or inventory levels. These values are important when making business decisions.

- *Internal balancing* involves checking values such as record counts, or run times. These values can be used to check the integrity of the processing.

Balancing Runs

Balancing is performed after a report is produced and before it reaches the end user. Balancing is performed to verify that the report is accurate. Balancing involves certain parts of the report being examined and the figures given being checked against expected values. This may involve values from two or more reports being checked. When the figures match, the report is said to be "in balance." When they do not match, the reports are said to be "out of balance."

At most sites, for most of the time, the reports are correct and the checking activity is a waste of time. However, every time the report is produced, the operators have to go through something similar to the following procedure:

- Examine current totals.

- Examine previous totals or brought-forward totals. These earlier totals may be from the same suite of jobs, from the previous running of the job, or from quite separate jobs.

- Perform some calculations, such as subtracting one total from another.

- Perform comparisons—the balancing rules.

- Follow special instructions, which specify what to do if the report does not balance.

Benefits

The benefits that can be derived from automating the balancing process can be summarized as:

- Improved service.
- Elimination of delays.
- Reduction in costs.
- Other.

Improved service

The balancing activity can be performed automatically to ensure that all reports reaching end users are correct. The error situations that may in the past have occurred because operators decided an out-of-balance report was correct, or an in-balance report was wrong are eliminated. End users get only good reports from the MIS department.

If a report is out of balance, the automation software will identify it, and the operations group can take the appropriate action to remedy the situation. Or better still, an additional program can perform the error-correcting activity. Again, this results in end users getting only correct reports.

If the operators are not spending their time balancing reports, they can be performing other tasks that are of value to the end users that previously the operators did not have time to do; alternatively the operator role can be removed.

Delay elimination

By using software rather than people to carry out the balancing of the reports can greatly reduce the amount of time taken. This reduction in time may make the company more competitive in business.

The other advantage associated with reduction in checking time is that, once the batch jobs are checked and correct, the on-line systems can be restarted. If a company can be more competitive because its CICS system, for example, is available for more of the day, then completing its batch work faster gives it a competitive edge. And many sites are attempting to offer 24-hour working with only the minimum amount when the full on-line service is not available.

Cost reduction

Many out-of-balance situations are a result of the wrong data having been supplied. By quickly identifying the problem, the job or the step can be rerun using the correct data. This reduces the impact on other dependent jobs. Savings are made in paper costs, human resources, and machine time because dependent jobs do not have to be rerun because an error was not identified by the operator.

Other

The other benefits that come from automated report balancing are:

- The correct procedure is always adopted; errors are eliminated.
- Staff absence (through illness or holiday) does not affect performance. The absence of the person who knows the right procedure to adopt is no longer a problem.
- Processing can be moved to a remote system without needing to move staff.

Automated Software Facilities

An automated balancing system should offer the following facilities:

- Automate balancing.
- Automate all current procedures.
- Ability for nonprogrammers to specify balancing rules.
- Verify information from outside sources.
- Allow future changes.
- Minimally impact operating system.

Automate balancing

The balancing activity involves the comparison of current totals with totals carried forward and calculated items. The software must allow the comparison between totals in the current cycle, and totals from a previous cycle. Older cycles' figures may be used in trend analysis investigations. The automation software should be able to retrieve historical data.

Allowing the software to perform the checks is a way of building quality control into the software. In the event of a fault being detected that the software cannot fix, it must be able to call someone to fix it or pass a message to an automated problem management system.

Automate all current procedures

The automation software chosen must be able to perform all the tasks currently performed by people.

Ability for nonprogrammers to specify balancing rules

The people who usually perform the balancing activity are rarely programmers. They are also, quite often, the only people who know exactly what the procedures are. Therefore, it is useful if the automation software has a user-friendly interface that allows these people to input their knowledge into the system.

Verify information from outside sources

Some balancing involves checking data from sources outside the suite of jobs producing the report. The automation software must be able to access data and verify data from other reports or files.

Allow future changes

Whatever automation package is selected, there is every likelihood of the automation system being developed further, and software must be able to incorporate these future changes. It is also likely that the balancing rules may be changed as a result of other changes within the company. These changes must also be taken into consideration.

Minimal impact on operating system

The automation software can have an impact on system performance that is much greater than originally anticipated unless care is taken to ensure that it does not impact on the operating system to any large extent. Ideally, the automation software should use minimal amounts of processor resources.

The automation software should, preferably, not have any hooks into the operating system, and the software should not require any changes to the programming of the jobs that are being balanced.

Batch Management

Batch management requires that certain processes are in place to support the automation. These processes include:

- *Operations standards:* Operators must know how to run systems and applications in the event that the automation software fails and also to ensure, in the first instance, that the automation software is working properly.

- *Acceptance testing:* Operations must accept only working systems. If there is a problem with the automation, it will make more work for operators and is likely to cause more errors.

- *Development phase reviews:* Operators must be involved early enough in the development life cycle to make sure that new services meet operability requirements.

- *Effective change management:* This is necessary to control the increasing number of changes that will be implemented.

14

Recovery and Restart

No matter how well implemented the automation system is, there will be occasions when something goes wrong and it is necessary to recover from that problem or restart. It may be necessary to restart either an application or the whole system. When thinking in terms of recovery and restart, it is important to also consider what to do in the event of the automation system's performing incorrectly or failing totally.

The areas that are considered in this chapter are:

- Application program failure.
- Subsystem failure.
- Operating system failure.
- Hardware failure.
- Network failure.
- Automation system failure.
- Automated problem management system failure.

Application Program Failure

After development work has been carried out, it is important to control the placement of programs and procedures into the correct production libraries. If this step is successfully carried out, it will remove one source of failure too often associated with running application programs.

Where there is a problem with a batch job, steps have to be taken to recover from the situation or, if it is unrecoverable, to alert humans using an automated problem management system. The tasks that usually have to be performed include dataset scratching, GDG adjusting, and JCL overrides. Good operators can usually identify a problem quickly, and immediately follow the appropriate procedure to overcome it. Automated systems operations software (scheduler software) should similarly take appropriate action immediately. The software may back out the changes that have been made by the failed job and/or restore files (and leave a message for a human), or it may automatically restart the job at the correct point in the JCL. All recovery jobs that may be used in the event of a batch job failure must be known to the scheduler.

An alternative way of overcoming problems with failing applications is to write application systems that have recovery routines built into them that will start automatically.

With an automatic problem management system, when a problem with a batch job occurs that cannot be fixed by the automation software, it is possible to call people immediately. If they are at home or at a remote site, they can use remote diagnostics by dialing up from a PC, and they can fix the problem.

Subsystem Failure

The loss of a major subsystem can have important consequences on a company in terms of lost revenue. It is vital that subsystem failures are automatically recovered quickly or, where this is not possible, the automatic problem management system is used to immediately call humans. An automation package should identify the outage and restart faster than a human can. While automation software within CICS can be used to overcome many CICS-related problems, it cannot cope if CICS itself crashes. In such cases, the automation software needs to be outside CICS.

CICS Version 2.1 has EXtended Recovery Feature (XRF). XRF has two identical versions of CICS running in two separate address spaces. One version is active, and one is dormant. The dormant copy periodically checks the status of the active version. If anything appears to be amiss, the dormant version takes over the workload. This reduces or eliminates any downtime. Since recovery is automated, failures are masked from the end user and do not require operator intervention. During takeover, XRF automatically transfers ownership of CICS disk based resources on shared DASD from the active to the alternative system. Back-out of in-flight tasks takes place before initialization of the alternative CICS system is complete. All active VTAM terminal sessions are reinstated.

The Remote Recovery Data Facility (RRDF) 1.2 is available for CICS, IMS, and DB2. It allows log data to be sent to an alternative site, thereby providing protection against catastrophic loss.

To identify subsystems that are failing, but that have not sent specific messages, the NetView Program-to-Program Interface (PPI) can be used. The PPI allows application programs to send generic alerts to NetView. This is done by writing an application program that CALLs module CNMNETV.

Operating System Failure

In a traditional MVS site, the loss of the MVS operating system would be immediately noticed by users, and would be fairly quickly identified by the operators who would take steps to perform a dump (if required) and restart the system. The big problem with a basic automation system is that the software will have been running in an MVS address space. If MVS is not running, the automation system cannot be running.

To overcome this problem, two alternatives are possible. The first option is a PC or PS/2 attached to the processor. The PC would perform regular handshaking with the processor (and indeed other activities). When the PC received no response from the mainframe, it would initiate the IPL procedure. The second option is to link to another mainframe. The second mainframe would notice the system failure on the first processor and perform the necessary IPL.

Once the operating system is reactivated, the automation system must takeover to restart all the subsystems and recover all the previously active batch jobs that had not completed before the crash. Scheduler software should know what jobs were running, and perform restart/rerun activities for them. To do this the scheduler will need checkpoint datasets.

Hardware Failure

In the event of a hardware component's failing, it is necessary for the monitoring software to identify that the component has failed and attempt to recover it. Some hardware failures will result in messages being generated, others may not. If the software cannot perform the recovery, the automated problem management system must be notified so that humans can be alerted.

NetView can respond when it receives a message, or it can issue display commands and react to the responses to the command. When a response to a display command is received, NetView can execute CLISTs or REXX EXECs. These CLISTs or REXX EXECs will obtain information from the control file and the status file, and will execute additional CLISTs or REXX EXECs to recover the failing resource. This kind of monitoring can be set to take place at fixed intervals (often 15 minutes).

When the hardware of the processor itself fails, it is useful if the automation system can transfer work from the failing processor to another. An automated problem management system can be used to tell humans that an engineer is required to fix the failing processor. OPC/ESA provides a restart mechanism on a stand-by system in a sysplex that is running OPC/ESA. During recovery it transfers processing work from the failing processor.

When there are not other processors in a sysplex, an out-board PC is probably the only way of alerting people to the failure (apart from irate phone calls from users to the Help Desk).

Network Failure

Most mainframe computers are at the center of huge networks linking other mainframes, midrange machines, and PCs. Very few end users appreciate the scale of the network that they are using. However, failure of part of the network is soon noticed by the end users affected, and their inability to carry out useful work can be financially detrimental to a company.

With VTAM and NetView, it is possible to automatically restart network resources and to automate many other aspects that previously required network operators.

Automated Network Operations/MVS (ANO/MVS) monitors VTAM messages coming through NetView and, based on those messages, automatically reactivates SNA resources or notifies the network operator that SNA resources have gone down. The product automates routine operator tasks such as manually logging problems in NetView's hardware monitor, keeping status logs, and automatically restarting equipment that has gone off line.

Automation System Failure

If part or all the automation software fails—for example, if the automation software fails to start all the IMS regions—the automated problem management system must be informed immediately so that people can be informed. It is not satisfactory to discover that the automation software has failed to perform a particular task hours after the task should have been performed. There must be a fall-back procedure so that any remaining operators know exactly what to do to manually start all the IMS regions. If the message suppression/console management system fails, it could mean plugging in some old consoles and reminding operators to start jobs at specified times. If the scheduler goes, it could mean an old-fashioned hand-written schedule, and some operators working overtime through the night.

When only part of the automation system has failed or is performing in an unexpected manner, it is important that the other components can continue to function successfully. It is also important that the failing components instructions can be overridden by the operator. In this way the system can be kept going until such time as the failing software component can be fixed.

When a single part of the automation software fails, it is a useful facility if the automation software can "catch up" once it is restarted. This means that it ought to be able to perform all the specified tasks that should have been performed by the automation software, but that were not performed, while the automation software was unavailable.

If all the automation system fails, the problem is how does the automation system tell the operators that it has failed? An ideal automation system would know that it had failed and would tell someone. One way of identifying that the automation has failed is if there is a task supervisor that checks on the automation. And if the logic is continued, it is necessary to have a task manager that will ensure that the task supervisor is functioning successfully. With NetView Release 2 and above, it is possible to have a small, separate region that would monitor the primary region for failures. And following the logic it would be necessary to have a small NetView region monitoring the region that monitors the primary region. These extra NetView regions could be used to restart the automation system.

If the automation software fails and cannot be restarted, sites are left with having to use humans until such time as the problem can be resolved and the automation software can take over. The solution to the problem must be incorporated into the automation software so that the same problem cannot happen again.

It is essential that, after the automation software is installed and running, people retain a knowledge of how the automation system works, what it is meant to achieve, and how to fix any problems that occur. If the whole automation software fails, a recovery plan must be in place to allow MIS service to still be offered to end users. In the past, sites have relied on exoperators working in other departments to come back to their old jobs and run the system. The disadvantages are that in the future there may not be enough exoperators to do the job, they may have forgotten much of what they knew, and the system may have changed out of all recognition (caused by new procedures made available by the automation software).

It is important to ensure that access to the automation software is secure so that it cannot be tampered with. If the automation software is corrupted, a secure back-up copy will have to be installed before the automation system can be used.

Automated Problem Management System Failure

Throughout the development of the automation system it is important to have an automated problem management system to notify the human operators that some automation task has not been performed successfully or some component of the system has failed that the automation software cannot recover. However, if people rely on the problem management system notifying them of problems, what is available to tell people if the problem management system itself fails?

The solution is similar to the one used when the automation system fails.

The automation system must be able to monitor the problem management system and must utilize a back-up system to inform people of the problem.

The automation system itself may be working quite happily for a long time after the automated problem management system fails, and so the failure of this component will not be noticed by irate end users.

15

Automated Systems Operations and CICS

IBM's Customer Information Control System (CICS) is a very popular transaction processing system. It runs under MVS and VSE, and there are also variants for VM, OS/2 (Operating System/2), and AIX on the RS/6000 called CICS/6000. There are certainly more MVS sites running CICS than are running IMS, IBM's other mainframe transaction processing system. This chapter looks at ways of automating CICS, although much of what is said is also applicable to IMS and similar systems.

Not only are more sites using CICS today than ever before, but also the sites that have it are making more use of it than ever before. A direct consequence of this to the MIS department is that the availability and performance of CICS need to be very high to satisfy the demands of the user departments. This is no easy task with increasing transaction volumes and a growing number of new applications.

At most sites, the way to make available to end users the highest level of CICS availability and performance is to automate the operation of CICS. As problems usually occur when the CICS system is running, and as processor speeds get faster, it becomes more and more important to solve the problems at machine speed rather than at people speed. IBM has itself announced a CICS automation product called CICS AO/MVS.

Reasons for Automating CICS Operations

The benefits to a site of automating CICS operations can be summarized as follows:

- Improved service.
- Increased availability of CICS.

- Fewer operator errors.
- Routine actions automated.
- Complex actions automated.
- Responses to problems automated.
- Problem diagnosis automated.
- Data collection automated.

Improved service

The level of service that the MIS department offers the end users is improved because operator mistakes are eliminated, all actions take place at machine speed rather than operator speed, and all time dependent activities take place at the correct time.

Increased availability

The availability of CICS can be increased by:

- Reducing MVS downtime.
- Reducing CICS region downtime.
- Improving availability of resources.

If MVS is performing badly, it makes no difference what changes are made to CICS, they will have no apparent effect. Once steps have been taken to improve MVS performance, CICS performance will also improve. If MVS performance is satisfactory, then work must be done on CICS.

It is possible to reduce CICS region downtime and improve the availability of resources in a number of ways. These include:

- Switching to alternative CICS address space.
- Automating CICS restart after a failure.
- Reducing the time taken to complete batch processing of on-line files.
- Improving transaction/resource availability.

Switching to alternative CICS address space.   With CICS 2.1 the EXtended Recovery Feature (XRF) allows a dormant CICS address space to take over CICS activity if the active CICS address space crashes for any reason. For more details see the section on XRF later in this chapter.

Automating CICS restart.   Even in the best planned data center unforeseen problems can occur. When automating, it is necessary to plan for the unexpected. Where a dormant address space is not used, restarting CICS must follow as soon after a crash as possible to minimize time lost. An automation package should identify the outage and restart faster than a human can.

Reducing batch run time.   The length of time taken by a batch job can be extended by the other events that have to occur. For example, it may be necessary to disable some terminals, and enable them after the batch job completes successfully. Batch jobs may take longer due to contention on files, disks, or channels. It may be possible to reduce batch run times by using a scheduling package to run the job at a different time of day and so reduce contention, thus speeding up the job. It should also be possible to automate some of the other events, such as issuing commands. Again this would reduce the total time taken. It takes longer to enter commands at a keyboard at human speed.

It is also a good idea to run certain jobs before the standard batch job. For example, before a batch job updating CICS files is run, another job could run checking that all the required files are closed and disabled on the on-line system. If a file was open, the automation software could send a message to the file's users asking them to complete their work and free the file. Alternatively, the job could schedule itself to run again in five minutes. It would keep checking every five minutes until all the resources were available, and then the batch job could run. This could be performed with a CLIST or a REXX EXEC.

Another use of automation software would be to check the error code in the event of the job failing. It would then try whatever corrective action had been programmed into it.

Batch processing run times can be reduced by automating job submission based on time of day, or in response to the completion of other prerequisite jobs or events. The automation software will be aware that one job has finished and will have started the next one, long before a human operator will have noticed the message saying that the first job has completed successfully.

Improving transaction availability.   For a transaction to process successfully, it must have available terminals, programs, and files or databases. It probably also needs MRO/ISC (MultiRegion Operation/InterSystem Communication) connections and other resources. If any of these are missing, a problem will occur. An automated operations package could monitor the availability of these resources and automatically restart them if they became unavailable. If a terminal was out of service, a CEMT command could be automatically issued to bring the terminal in service. If it was a VTAM problem, the automated operations package could issue a VTAM command to reactivate the terminal, then a further command would be issued to acquire the terminal for CICS.

Reducing operator errors

Operators frequently get blamed for many problems, some of which are not their fault at all. However, operator errors that are likely to cause downtime are:

- *Keystroke errors:* A command is miskeyed and has to be rekeyed.

- *Memory lapses:* The operator cannot remember the syntax of the command or the appropriate command. In this case time is lost while the operator consults the manuals.

- *Procedural errors:* Complex procedures are incorrectly followed. This again loses time as manuals are consulted.

Automated software can be used to regularly monitor the system and automatically issue commands to bring failing components back in service. This will eliminate many of the problems just listed. Automation software can also be used to start jobs such as journal back-ups. The automation software will not forget what the start command is, when to start it, or even that it needs to be started.

Automated operations software can also be used for message suppression. The operator sitting at the master terminal will not have the important messages masked by a barrage of trivia.

Automating routine actions

In an ideal world, operators would give the master terminal their undivided attention. They would automatically start transactions at the time appointed, and they would know exactly what was happening from reading each message as it appeared.

In the real world, automated operations software can be used to perform time-dependent activities, such as starting transactions.

Automating complex actions

More complex actions, such as backing up journals, could also be automated. When a journal dataset is full, CICS sends a message to the master terminal asking that the operator copy the journal, and that the operator reply to the outstanding message when the copy is complete. The operator will see the message, start the copy job, and answer the message when it has successfully completed.

The process can be automated by using a CLIST that will respond to the DFH4583 message and copy the journal. A second CLIST can be used to check that the first has completed successfully and to answer the outstanding message.

Automating response to problems

Automation software can also perform situation-specific activities because it does not get tired of routine monitoring activities. An example would be a transaction in a loop that was using all the storage in the DSA (dynamic storage area). This situation could crash CICS in less than a minute. The automation software could detect the high usage of storage (short-on-storage message DFH0506) and could monitor for transactions using very large amounts of storage in very short periods of time. The problem transaction could be cancelled and the short-on-storage situation avoided.

Automating problem diagnosis

Most CICS performance monitors issue messages warning of existing or potential performance problems. The automation software can be used to take appropriate action. If the problem reported is not straightforward, it is useful if the automation software can request additional information from the monitor to clarify the problem and act on this information.

Automating data collection

If problems occur that the automation software is unable to deal with directly, it should request a trace and collect additional data automatically. It should also ensure that key personnel are alerted. Examples might include excessive VSAM CI/CA (Control Interval/Control Area) splits, string waits, buffer waits, and excessive short-on-storage occurrences.

CICS Automation Features

Now available are a number of software facilities from IBM that perform some of the activities that would be performed by automated operations software.

EXtended Recovery Feature

CICS Version 2 Release 1 introduced the EXtended Recovery Feature (XRF). This is available for MVS users and VSE users. XRF facilitates continuous CICS operation and unattended operation.

XRF requires two identical versions of CICS to be running in two separate address spaces. One version is active, and one is dormant. The dormant copy periodically checks the status of the active version. If anything appears to be amiss, the dormant version takes over the workload. This reduces or eliminates any downtime. Since recovery is automated, failures are masked from the end user and do not require operator intervention.

Automatic takeover can be triggered by:

- CICS failure.
- VTAM failure.
- Operating system failure.
- CEC failure.
- Operator command.

The operator command is:

CEMT PERFORM SHUTDOWN TAKEOVER

During takeover, XRF automatically transfers ownership of CICS disk-based resources on shared DASD from the active to the alternative system. Back-out of in-flight tasks takes place before initialization of the alternative CICS system is complete. All active VTAM terminal sessions are reinstated.

The PR/SM (Processor Resource/System Manager) feature can be used to provide a resilient environment either between CECs or on a single serial number for CICS. Hot stand-by in a multi-CEC configuration takes an estimated four to five minutes for 1000 CICS terminals. Hot stand-by in a single CEC offer less protection against physical catastrophe, but recovery times are considerably shorter.

Under PR/SM, production CICS and a monitor program can be run in one logical partition while the stand-by task, with its own monitor, runs in a separate partition. When the stand-by monitor no longer receives acknowledgments from the production monitor, it assumes that production CICS has failed and takes over.

On ES/9000 processors recovery of "in-flight" transactions is possible by backing them out of processor cache if the failing processor has any latent capacity.

Remote Recovery Data Facility

Remote Recovery Data Facility (RRDF), Version 1 Release 2, is available for IMS and DB2 as well as CICS. It is a remote site recovery offering that provides realtime electronic transmission of log data to an alternative site, thereby providing protection against catastrophic loss.

CICS Automation Option/MVS

The CICS Automation Option/MVS (CICS AO/MVS) provides a single point of control for CICS operations based on the automation environment provided by AOC/MVS (Automated Operations Control/MVS) or Automated Console Operations (ACO) SolutionPac. IBM claims that it has all the user benefits associated with automation such as automated start-up, shutdown, and recovery.

CICS AO/MVS works with NetView and responds automatically to a range of alerts and events across the network. A network manager can control and monitor a network of multiple CICS regions from a single console. Functions that are automated include system start-up, shutdown, and recovery.

CICS AO/MVS monitors LU6.1 and LU6.2 links that support CICS sessions. The monitor tries to reacquire a session when a link goes down, and notifies ACO if the attempt fails. It can also reacquire links that were cut off as a result of NCP (network control program) failure.

CICS AO/MVS provides dynamic color-coded graphic description of the changing status of a VTAM network.

Users need to set up a rule-based repository (part of the system) to tell the automation system how to react.

IMS Automation Option/MVS

For sites that are using IMS rather than CICS, there is a product called Information Management System Automation Option for MVS (IMS AO/MVS). IMS AO/MVS controls multiple local or remote IMS regions by automating functions usually performed by the operator. This eliminates the need for an operator for each of these regions. The product monitors LU2-based interregion communications and intersystem communications between IMS regions to help:

- Reduce unplanned outages.

- Optimize planned outages.

- Consolidate a multitude of commands into single directives issued from the NetView console.

IMS AO/MVS is meant to simplify resource management in distributed environments by coordinating functions and eliminating redundancy. IMS AO/MVS can work with IMS XRF (EXtended Recovery Facility) to transfer the primary IMS system to a back-up system without interrupting operations. The whole process is meant to be transparent to the end user.

A rules-based repository, which comes with the product, is used to define how the automation product is to react to specified situations. It requires AOC/MVS or NetView ACO SolutionPac.

16

Automated Systems
Operations and Monitors

All MVS sites make use of some kind of monitor. In fact, performance monitoring is an activity that was taking place at MVS sites long before any thought was given to its role in automated systems operations.

Performance monitors can generally be divided into two categories. There are realtime monitors that measure specific resources and report immediately. They are frequently used by operators for problem determination. The other category of monitors are historical monitors that record the state of the system at various intervals. These records are available for later analysis.

It is the first type of monitor that can be linked with automated systems operations software. Once the monitor has identified a problem or a potential problem, the automation software can take the prescribed steps to recover from the problem. In this situation there is no need for the monitor software to produce color graphics of what is going on because the aim of the automation process is to remove the need for the operator to get involved. However, while the automation is being implemented, the operator will need to monitor system performance.

Performance Monitoring

Performance monitors are software that run on the system they are monitoring. One consequence of this is that the system will not perform so well because machine cycles, etc., are being taken up by the monitor software rather than by other work. Monitors can either come on at certain times of day or they can be active the whole time. Many sites do not use their monitor during periods of peak workflow because the resources used by the monitor slow everything else down. This is usually the period that needs to be monitored the most, because tuning could probably be most beneficial at this time.

A monitor that is on all the time can be used to tell the operator how the system is performing. It can alert the operator to any threshold values being reached. More sophisticated performance monitors can identify a problem and take the predetermined steps to solve the problem.

It is possible, using a PC and an IRMA board, for example, to log on to the mainframe from a PC and monitor what is going on. It is even possible to run "batch" jobs on the PC that monitor the mainframe and will alert the PC operator if jobs fail, or to automatically issue start commands, such as Start IMS, if all the batch jobs complete successfully.

Performance Reporting

It is important to know how the system is performing. For one thing, users demand it. For another, it is impossible to know if a change has improved performance unless reports of system performance before and after the change are available.

Reports assume that monitoring information is stored. This historical monitoring information can be used to identify trends and for capacity planning. It can also be used to show users that Service Level Agreements (SLAs) are being met or even exceeded.

Automated Problem Management System

In the early stages, before the monitor and automation software are sophisticated enough to deal with all contingencies, there will be occasions when an event occurs that the automation system is not prepared to handle. In these circumstances an automated problem management system is required to take control. The problem management system can be used to:

- Request help from an appropriate person.
- Request help at an appropriate time.
- Request additional help if the problem persists.

The problem management system must "know":

- Whom to contact.
- When to contact them.
- How to contact them.
- What to do if they cannot be contacted.

The system must be flexible. People may want to go on holiday for a week (a new contact name and number must be used on these occasions), or even out for the evening (different contact numbers are required for different times of day).

It might be useful if the automated problem management system was sophisticated enough that the Help Desk and even end users were informed of the problem!

Automated System Monitoring

Automated system monitoring offers the following facilities:

- Allows the definition of normal parameters for response time, CPU utilization, resource utilization, elapsed time, etc.

- Provides an on-line diagnostic tools for problem identification.

- Provides data for historical analysis.

- Identifies the current processing status of the system and can reallocate resources to specified work.

- Identifies when site-specified thresholds are reached and takes remedial action.

At the simplest level, it is possible to automate responses to certain messages as they are sent from different system and subsystem components. Some of these messages can be used to trigger responses automatically, because operators would respond in a particular way when they saw it. For example, IEF450I JOB ABENDED indicates a job failure or system component failure. Most sites will retry the job before calling technical support. This can be automated. In addition, the response of the technical support department can be automated.

IST020I VTAM INITIALIZATION COMPLETE indicates that VTAM is up, and is usually the cue that operators need to start TSO. Again this can be easily automated.

IEE043I indicating that the system log is full can be used to automatically trigger writing the log to DASD.

In addition to simply monitoring the messages from the systems and various subsystems, it is possible to respond to messages from the system monitor.

When first automating monitoring, it is useful to keep a count of how often exception conditions are reported. At this stage it is important to ensure that the threshold values set in the monitor really do indicate an error.

The next step is to define a policy regarding the action to be taken when exception conditions occur. For example, if CPU is less than 50 percent for more than five minutes, the TSO MAXUSER level could be raised and another initiator started. Or if TSO response times exceed one second for more than ten minutes the IEAIPS member in use could be changed so that short TSO transactions are favored.

Once the policies are decided, they should be implemented using the automation software.

If more than one monitor is used—such as a system monitor, a subsystem monitor, and a network monitor—the information must be brought together, and a common presentation format for the data should be used before presentation to the automation software or the operator console.

All data being picked up by the various monitors should be filtered and only important information passed on. This information can be highlighted if being presented to an operator or acted on by automation software. If the automation software cannot deal with the problem identified, an operator should be alerted (paged).

The trigger to perform an activity can be based on threshold levels being exceeded, and CLISTs or REXX procedures can be called to perform the actions.

With monitor software it is possible to perform actions that the operator might try to do, but usually fails due to other work that has to be performed. For example, the monitor software can be used to monitor VTAM nodes, terminals, and applications. It can monitor JES2 lines, and it can monitor CICS tasks for hangs. The software might, for example, issue commands every ten minutes to find the status of devices and the like. If a fault is detected as a result of the response to a command, appropriate steps to fix the fault can be taken automatically.

In terms of response, not only should the monitor software respond to failures of components (standard fire-fighting techniques), but it should also take preventive steps to ensure that failures do not occur.

There is a potential problem in building a monitor that reacts in response to messages from systems and subsystems. This is because the messages may change with new releases of the software. Therefore, the automated monitor should respond to status indications for each component which it must identify itself.

When anyone looks at the monitor, it would be useful if the information was presented using icons. So, for example, an icon of a tape drive could be used to represent each tape drive, or a symbol for a modem could be used, and so on. The performance of each component being monitored could be color coded. In this way, human monitoring would simply require someone to check that all icons were color-coded green, for example, and anything color-coded red was a failing or failed component. The monitor should be able to identify any component that was under pressure and perhaps likely to fail, and this could be color-coded amber. If people do not like the use of icons, it is possible to color code messages. It is useful if these messages are understandable rather than the raw system message.

Network monitors

In addition to system monitors there are a number of network performance monitors available. These can be used to ensure that the network is performing optimally, and should be linked with system monitors as part of the automation process.

The main network monitors in use by MVS sites are listed in Appendix B.

Future Problems

Monitoring a single MVS system has associated problems, but these will seem simple and easy to resolve in comparison to the problems that sites are likely to experience in the near future. A problem that some sites are beginning to experience is one where IBM hardware is linked to computers from other suppliers, such as DEC and Hewlett-Packard. With the growth in automation software, it is often the case that these other systems are controlled from the MVS console or from the MVS automation software. If an end user requests a file which is located on one of the other computers, and their screen remains blank for a long time, they will want to know what caused the delay. The monitor in use must be able to identify the cause of the delay, whether it was between the terminal and the MVS system, between the MVS system and the "other platform" or on the "other platform." Not only must the monitor report on more areas in the future (i.e., outside the IBM hardware), but also it must take appropriate action to overcome the problem.

Candle Corporation, for example, has announced that its Enterprise Availability Monitoring services package allows users on an MVS mainframe to monitor DEC and Tandem hardware as well.

Similarly, the growth in the number of PCs and workstations connected through an LAN to an MVS mainframe causes monitoring problems. The monitor needs to be able to monitor each component between the end user and the application on the mainframe being used. The monitor must again identify any poorly performing component and either report on its performance or take action to overcome the problem.

Environmental Monitors

In a lights-out situation, where there are no people near the hardware, it is important to have monitors that can report on various ambient conditions, such as temperature and humidity. It is very useful indeed if these monitors can be linked into the automation software. In the event of a monitor identifying a problem, the automation software can ensure that humans are alerted, via its automated problem management system, and also take any steps necessary to facilitate recovery, such as shutting on-line systems and switching work to alternative processors. If key cards are used to identify who has entered the computer area, it is possible for the automation system to be aware if any humans are around. If none are, it could trigger the halon gas system, for example, to start immediately to put out a fire. Sites may have to purchase new sensors that can be linked to the automation system.

17

Automated Systems Operations and the Network

It is not possible for all the user terminals and other peripheral devices to be directly attached to the mainframe. A 37xx communication controller is usually attached to a channel attached to the mainframe. Attached to the communications controller are modems. Using phone lines, end users can connect to the communications controller. This represents the physical network.

Running inside the communications controller is the NCP (network control program). The NCP is software that performs many of the functions that otherwise would have to be performed by the mainframe software. Running in the mainframe is VTAM (virtual telecommunications access method). VTAM manages session establishment and data flow between terminals and application programs.

At any site where the network is getting bigger, there are more tasks to perform. As the number of tasks increases, so does the complexity of the system. With the increase in complexity, the likelihood of error also increases. As with all automation of the operator's function, there will be an increase in the serviceability, availability, and reliability of the system resulting from automated network operations. The automation allows the operator to escape from the mundane and to perform higher-level functions.

Traditionally, network operators are expected to monitor network resources, start and stop diagnostic traces, recover failed resources, and look after communication controllers (dump/load/restart). Automation software should be capable of taking over these tasks.

Software Choices

The automation technique that is chosen by a site must depend on that site's needs and the available resources. It should be borne in mind that if the automation tool is swapped out by MVS because of MVS's priorities, the automation tool will be more or less useless. It is possible to run an automation tool that is external to the system.

Available software includes:

- High-Level Language Application Programming Interface (HLLAPI) from IBM-PC options.
- DREAM from Grand Metropolitan.
- Automator "mi" from Direct Technology.
- Net/Master from Systems Center.
- NetView, or on older systems, its component Network Communications Control Facility (NCCF) from IBM.

The first three products in the list can be used to run the automation tool externally from the system. One possible method is to adopt a PC-based approach. It is possible to use a channel attached PC (286 or above) running distributed function terminal (DFT) communications software (non-IBM), which provides MVS console access and three SNA sessions. This can be driven by, for example, Automator "mi."

For many sites, the only choice is to use the Automated Network Operations feature available with NetView from IBM.

Planning for Automation

Tasks performed at a data center can be divided into five categories:

- Manual.
- Consistent.
- Investigative.
- Time-dependent.
- Unnecessary.

Manual tasks

Manual tasks are ones that require some kind of human activity, such as loading a tape. If an alternative is possible (for example, putting datasets on disk rather than tape), the task can be retained as one that could be automated. If there is no easy alternative, the task should be removed from the list of those to be automated.

Consistent tasks

Consistent tasks are those that occur after an event on the network has occurred. The response is consistently the same each time the event occurs. These tasks can usually be automated by CLISTs in a NetView automation table.

Investigative tasks

Investigative tasks are ones that the operator undertakes to determine the cause of a problem. They usually involve commands asking for status displays and for the analysis of these displays. These types of tasks are typically handled by NetView timers, and may be handled by message handlers in the automation table.

Time-dependent tasks

Time-dependent tasks are tasks that always occur at a particular time of day or on a particular day. These tasks can usually be automated by simple task schedulers or NetView timers.

Unnecessary tasks

Inertia can occur at any time, at any level. Tasks are sometimes done in a particular way because they have always been done in a particular way, irrespective of whether this is the best way. Some tasks performed at a site have just "grown up" over the years. One advantage of automation is that these tasks can be clearly identified and eliminated. The unnecessary tasks are not automated, they are eliminated.

Problems

The move to network automation is fraught with problems, and every site that has undergone the process can regale you with horror stories. An example is a site that was using NetView Release 1 and found that NetView intermittently stopped detecting messages. The problem, in fact, was solved by a VTAM PTF (program temporary fix) that repaired the message handler.

Other problems can occur with the introduction of new releases of existing software, and with the introduction of entirely new pieces of software. For example, one site had to completely stop its use of PC-based support after the introduction of Release 3 of NPM (NetView Performance Monitor).

Controlling Automation

It is the network operators who will be freed up from their more mundane tasks by the introduction of automation, and it is also the network operators who will have to supervise the running of the automation software initially. Additionally it is they who will have to step in should the automation software fail. The first law of programming says that any software will go as much awry as the programming language allows. One way of enhancing NetView network automation software is to make the on-line help facilities more accessible and more easily maintainable. This makes it easier for the operators to find the information they need in order to track down problems.

Should on-line recovery be impossible, it is necessary to resort to change removal. Change control is essential to allow assured removal or back-out of any changes made. Not only must the network automation system be fully implemented, it must be well understood.

Any change control technique must be independent of the failing software. This means that if the problem is with NetView, for example, NetView CLIST logic or NetView functions should not be used. The most satisfactory technique is probably to use standard MVS utilities.

Automated Network Operations for MVS

IBM has announced that Automated Network Operations/MVS (ANO/MVS) works with NetView Version 1.3 or above to provide an automated network operations management system for MVS/XA and MVS/ESA environments. The program presents a dynamic, color status display of the network components, full-screen operator interface, improved NCP recovery, automation availability reports, X.25 support, and platform support for automation extension by customers. It replaces NetView ANO.

The Future

The future will see an increase in the use of LANs (local area networks) attached to the mainframe. These will be used by end users and will be available to operators. Operators will be able to use a PC or PS/2 to assess the system and to run support and information tools. The use of expert systems will increase, and these will help automate actions currently performed manually. At the moment it is possible to use knowledge-based systems to advise operators during recovery activities. In the future operators could use home-based terminals to perform activities such as re-IPL of systems out of hours.

Net/Master

The main competitor to IBM's NetView is Net/Master from Systems Center. It is marketed as a strategy for network and system management. The base product, which is called Net/Master Foundation (NMF), provides users with a single console image of their system and includes a 4GL and a security system. Associated with Net/Master are:

- Network/Master, which provides network operations management.

- SYS/Master, which is the component in charge of automated operations.

- INFO/Master, which looks after problem, change, configuration, and inventory management.

- Network DataMover, which provides facilities for data transfer.

The Net/Master product range allows network management across multiple hardware platforms.

The October 1991 issue of *The IBEX Bulletin** found that 87 percent of sites with a network management package have NetView and 13 percent have Net/Master. However, Net/Master users rated their product more highly than NetView users.

The IBEX Bulletin is a monthly survey of IBM mainframe and compatible sites throughout the world. It is published by Xephon plc.

18

Automated Systems Operations and NetView

NetView was designed to act as the central network management facility for the SNA (systems network architecture) network. It was originally an agglomeration of existing products: NCCF (Network Communication Control Facility), NPDA (Network Problem Determination Application), and NLDM (Network Logical Data Manager). All SNA components, including all PUs (physical units) and LUs (logical units), maintain a session with an SSCP (System Services Control Point) in ACF/VTAM (Advanced Communication Function/Virtual Telecommunications Access Method). This allows NetView users to issue network management commands that can be passed to the SSCP that would then route the command to the required NAU (network addressable unit).

NetView now has two distinct and separate roles. It is IBM's vehicle for automated operations [AOC/MVS (Automated Operations Control/MVS)] as well as automated network management [ANO/MVS (Automated Network Operations/MVS)].

NetView is separate from VTAM. Users typically have two NetViews running: one attached to VTAM performing network management activities, and the other, via a link to the subsystem interface (SSI), performing automated operations functions.

NetView and Open Network Management Architecture

IBM's method of managing a network is the Open Network Management Architecture (ONMA). Its aims are to provide an architecture that:

- Encompasses all SNA products.
- Can connect to non-SNA systems.

■ This results in an architecture made up of concentric circles. They are the focal point, the entry point, and the service point (see Fig. 18.1).

At the center is the focal point containing NetView. This manages and controls the network. The focal point system and its back-up can run ISCF (InterSystem Control Facility) and ACA (Automated Console Applications), or TSCF (Target System Control Facility).

The *entry point* consists of products that link to the focal point using SNA. The products can be controlled from the focal point. Devices connected downstream from the entry point are SNA components and are controllable from the focal point.

Service point products are similar to entry point products, except that the downstream devices are not necessarily addressable from the focal point and do not use SNA protocols. An example of a service point is NetView/PC.

The *focal point* is the point at which statistics for the network can be derived.

Some non-SNA devices, such as those connected over an X.25 packet switched data network, require simulated LUs which are provided by the software interfacing with the X.25 network. Each virtual circuit is mapped onto an LU-LU session by NPSI (NCP packet switching interface) so that ACF/VTAM and the host application LU can view these non-SNA devices as either switched or nonswitched SDLC (synchronous data link control) devices. However, the simulated LUs are unable to participate in the Open Network Management Architecture as each LU is associated with a simulated PU type 1. PU type 1 peripheral nodes cannot accept or issue network management commands.

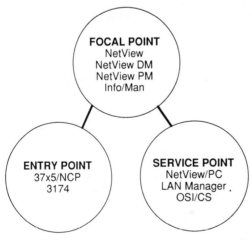

Figure 18.1. NetView architecture.

In a multihost network (i.e., many CPUs, each running VTAM and NetView), one NetView is defined as the focal point NetView. The other NetViews are not required to provide the complete management and reporting facilities of the focal point NetView. For example, it may not be necessary to configure the Hardware Monitor component of NetView, if that NetView has very few hardware components to monitor.

The benefits from running separate NetViews on the same system are:

- Separation of network management and automated operations facilities.

- Separation of local and remote systems.

- Resilience.

- Recovery.

NetView is not cheap and imposes a substantial logging overhead in large networks.

NetView Communications

NetView allows the combination of the MVS operator's console and the network operator's console. Management and control of the total system operation can be achieved using NetView. In order to do this, NetView makes use of SSI (SubSystem Interface) and Cross Memory Services (XMS).

SubSystem Interface

In order that NetView can receive messages destined for the operator's console and allow the NetView console operator to send system operator commands, there is an interface between NetView and MVS. This interface, called the SubSystem Interface (SSI), is illustrated in Fig. 18.2

The SSI is not formally documented because it is internal to the operating system. It consists of a message pathway that accepts messages from any software that is defined to MVS as a subsystem, for example, JES2, CICS, OPC/A (Operations Planning and Control/Advanced) or OPC/ESA (Operations Planning and Control/Enterprise Systems Architecture). A subsystem is defined to MVS by including its name in the SubSystem Name Table (SSNT), PARMLIB member IEASSNxx.

Originally the SSI was meant to be used with routing codes so that messages from these subsystems would be sent to the appropriate console. Messages requiring tape mounts would go to the tape library console, messages about print files would go to the printer's console or elsewhere. Messages placed on the SSI are available to all subsystems defined in the SSNT. The order in which each subsystem can examine a message on the SSI depends on the order that subsystems are placed in the SSNT.

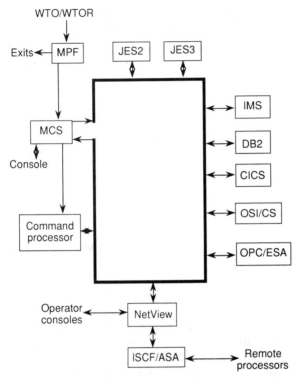

Figure 18.2. SubSystem Interface (SSI).

NetView Release 1 was not defined as a subsystem; so it did not have access to the SSI. The only way that the NetView console operator could interact with the MVS operator's console was by using WTO and WTOR messages.

Release 2 of NetView made it a subsystem that could be placed in the SSNT and that could read all the messages.

Release 2 of NetView also meant that OCCF (Operator Communications Control Facility) was no longer required. OCCF ran under NCCF (Network Communications Control Facility) allowing one or more remote systems to be operated from a host system over an SNA network. In effect, OCCF redirects operating system messages from remote sites to the managing site's operator console.

Figure 18.3 illustrates message routing and the NetView SSI. Figure 18.4 shows message routing in NetView.

Cross memory services

It is not sufficient to simply define NetView as a subsystem because NetView requires that VTAM is active. If there are problems with VTAM

MVS

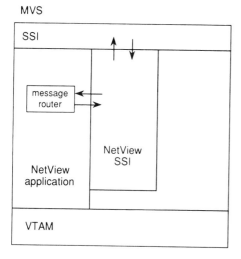

Figure 18.3. Message routing and
NetView SSI.

this may not be the case. One solution is to run multiple NetViews under a
single host, with one NetView defined as the subsystem and not dependent on VTAM for its operation. This NetView is often called the NetView
subsystem or automation NetView, while the NetView linked to VTAM is
the NetView application or network NetView.

As two NetViews exist it is necessary for them to be linked. This is done
using Cross Memory Services (XMS).

By using XMS and SSI it is possible for an operator logged on to the
NetView application to issue JES commands and receive the replies back
from JES.

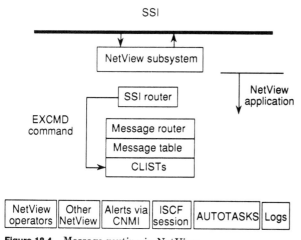

Figure 18.4. Message routing in NetView.

NetView Components

The main components of VTAM that can be used for automation are AUTOTASKs and global variables.

AUTOTASKs

Release 2 of NetView saw the introduction of AUTOTASKs. AUTO-TASKs permit the majority of the automation that is possible with Net-View. An AUTOTASK is similar to the Operator Station Task, that is associated with each logged-on console user, but it does not have a terminal. A VM user would think of this as being like a disconnected virtual machine.

For each AUTOTASK defined, there can be a CLIST or REXX EXEC running. These CLISTs can all be executing concurrently. One other advantage of AUTOTASKs is that they do not need VTAM to be active because they do not need a logged-on terminal.

Global variables

Global variables, a feature of NetView, are variables that can be accessed by multiple CLISTs. If the value of a global variable reaches a predetermined threshold value, a particular action can occur. For example, if an SSCP-PU session fails, a CLIST is invoked that issues the appropriate VTAM commands to activate the session to the PU. However, in the event of a major network failure, such as a power failure at a telephone repeater station, this may not be the most appropriate action. It is likely that a number of similar messages will be received, all causing a CLIST that will try starting the session. The better method is to use global variables to keep count of the number of times a particular CLIST is used or the number of VTAM failure messages being received. Once the threshold value is reached, operators could be warned, or more advanced procedures could be adopted.

NetView SolutionPac

NetView SolutionPac came with ACO (Automated Console Operations), and ANO (Automated Network Operations). ACO has since been replaced by AOC/MVS and ANO by ANO/MVS. NetView SolutionPac is still in use at many sites, which is why it is discussed here.

ACO automates:

■ IPL.

■ Shutdown of applications and the whole system.

■ Recovery of applications and subsystems.

ANO provides AHED (Automated HElp Desk), which offers a step-by-step guide for problem determination and tries to perform error recovery. Threshold values can be set to avoid certain overheads when trying to recover unrecoverable resources.

Automation Network Operations/MVS monitors VTAM messages coming through NetView and, based on those messages, automatically reactivates SNA resources or notifies the network operator that SNA resources have gone down. The product automates routine operator tasks such as manually logging problems in NetView's hardware monitor, keeping status logs, and automatically restarting equipment that has gone off line. It is meant to replace NetView ANO.

Automated Operations Console/MVS is a NetView application that automates some console operation functions. Available facilities include:

- Automated response to console messages.
- Operator usable dialogues.
- Realtime data store for automation.
- Operator-friendly interfaces for installation.

There are three types of files associated with this:

- Control file.
- Status file.
- Automation log.

Control file

The control file, a member of the NetView PARMLIB (EHKCFGxx), contains definitions required to manage the automated environment. It includes threshold values for recovery and the definitions of all subsystems and applications with their dependencies and recovery options.

Status file

The status file contains the automation status of each resource controlled by NetView, which can be retrieved by an operator command.

Automation log

The automation log contains only records related to automation.

NetView and Automation

NetView offers a variety of techniques that can be used for automation:

- Message suppression.
- Console consolidation.
- Alert issue.
- Message response.
- Time-dependent command issue.
- Application startup.

Messages coming from MVS can be filtered using MPF (Message Processing Facility, discussed in Chap. 10) and then passed through SSI to NetView. The message automation table is scanned to determine what action to perform—for example, issue an MVS command, execute a CLIST, or reroute the message. Additional suppression using global variables or output from display commands can be performed. The message automation table must be filled in by each site.

NetView Version 2.2 introduced management service units (MSUs). MSUs are better able to be used to respond to alerts than simple messages. They make it easier to automatically diagnose problems and then carry out recovery activities.

NetView can be used to consolidate consoles. Messages from many operating systems (e.g., MVS/ESA) can be consolidated on one console by using NetView-to-NetView (NNT) sessions. An automation task creates an NNT to collect message alerts from the network NetView. A focal point alert operator creates NNT sessions to gather alerts from other automation NetViews (on other processors). The NNT sessions are also used for commands by the operator and automation software.

At most sites, network operators are expected still to exist for the immediate future. NetView can send alerts to them when it detects a problem. There are two ways of doing this. One way allows only 11 lines of held messages to be available, which means that later, perhaps more important, messages will not be displayed. Alerts can be deleted using WTO and DOM. Most sites use the alternative method of generic alerts (GENALERTs) and the NPDA alerts on dynamic screens (see later in this chapter).

NetView can respond to messages. It issues an appropriate command from the automation table. More complex automation is possible with NetView Release 3 because REXX is available which is more powerful than CLISTs. It makes use of global variables.

NetView timers can be used to:

- Check that lines and clusters are active prior to on-line application starting.
- Send messages if start is late (e.g., CICS start).
- Remind operators of manual procedures.

- Perform sequencing automation (e.g., "Do this in five seconds").
- NetView can be used to start system tasks and applications, such as CICS.

A second NetView address space can be used to run all other NetView tasks, such as:

- Network automation.
- ANO (on the network owning system).
- Network subtasks (Session, hardware, and status monitors).
- Operations Help Desk.
- RTM (realtime monitor) can send data to SMF (system management facility).
- NPDA.

NetView can issue commands to ACF/VTAM. The operator can invoke CLISTs or REXX EXECs to generate VTAM commands. The command facility makes use of the Program Operator Interface into VTAM.

Responding to messages

It is possible for messages sent to the console to go unnoticed for long periods of time. If messages require an immediate human response, it is possible to send those to an operator console or to the Help Desk. The console must be associated with the NCCF part of NetView. Message routing requires entries in the message table to be coded. This also gives the opportunity for messages to be reworded so that they make sense to a normal human being. It is also possible to specify an audible alarm for some messages, or that they should be held on screen.

NPDA. The NPDA part of NetView provides for messages to be highlighted or for audible alarms to sound. The NPDA screen will roll the last alert off the screen as soon as the next alert arrives.

Message processing

The automation facilities available with NetView are similar to those used with MVS in terms of message suppression and filtering. Messages arriving at the NetView subsystem are inspected to see if further processing can take place in NetView. If not, the message is returned to the SSI. If yes, the message is next passed to the NetView application. Here it is received by a message router, which can invoke a CLIST or REXX EXEC. This is done using the EXCMD command. The appropriate EXCMD depends on the message.

If the message cannot be associated with an EXCMD command, the message table is checked. The message table contains entries relating to various message identities and other selection criteria. The entry indicates which NetView task the message should be routed to for processing. Messages may be logged with no further action occurring. Messages may be routed to an operator task so that it is displayed on the console.

The Program-to-Program Interface (PPI) allows application programs to send generic alerts to NetView. This is done by writing an application program that invokes module CNMNETV using the CALL statement. If, for example, a CICS problem occurs, module CNMNETV is called; this passes the alert to NetView which builds a dynamic alert screen.

NetView and Performance

There are two main aspects to NetView performance: the performance of NetView within its address space, and the performance of NetView's message processing facility.

NetView address spaces and performance

ANO and AOC can run in one NetView address space or in separate NetView address spaces. If ANO activity is typically high, AOC activity is typically low because it controls fewer resources. Also the likelihood of an application failure is less than the likelihood of a network failure. However, as AOC controls all subsystems and applications, including some MVS system components, AOC must have a high enough priority in the system to recover from any critical situation.

If ANO and AOC are run in the same address space they have to be given a high enough priority to ensure that AOC is effective, but the majority of the resources will be used by ANO performing less critical actions. This impacts on the production environment. Therefore, it is probably better to give ANO an address space with a lower priority, and AOC an address space with a higher priority.

Message flow and performance

Messages not suppressed by MPF are passed to NetView. This can be resource consuming (e.g., extra I/O) if NetView is not going to do anything with the message. It is possible to modify the MPF tables so that only messages explicitly defined in the table are routed to NetView. If this method is adopted, care must be taken when maintaining the tables, and some messages that may not be required in terms of NetView automation may be required to be written to the NetView log.

NetView's performance can be improved by taking care over the order of entries in its message table. The software does a sequential search of the table for each message. Therefore, more frequently used messages should be near the beginning.

NetView and Monitoring

NetView can respond when it receives a message, or it can issue display commands and react to the responses to the command. When a response to a display command is received, NetView executes CLISTs or REXX EXECs. These CLISTs or REXX EXECs will obtain information from the control file and the status file, and will execute additional CLISTs or REXX EXECs to recover the failing resource. This is a very CPU- and I/O-intensive activity. This kind of monitoring can be set to take place at fixed intervals. The length of these intervals can have an impact on performance. They should not be too close together or processor resources are wasted. They should not be too far apart, or the failing component will have sent a message and the active monitoring will be rendered unnecessary. Many sites consider that 15 minutes is probably the best interval.

Each CLIST that is used has to be read in from disk, translated, and executed. Because so many CLISTs are executed, this can result in a lot of I/O. To reduce the I/O and improve performance, the LOADCL command can be used. This will load CLISTs permanently into memory. The trade-off, of course, is that the amount of memory available for other processing is reduced. The CLISTs that could be loaded into memory are those that are most frequently used. The LOADCL command can be included in CNME1032. This is a member of the NetView CLIST library and is the startup CLIST for automated operator task AUTO1, which is executed at NetView initialization. To control the CLISTs that are loaded into memory, the MAPCL command can be used. CLISTs can be dropped from memory using the DROPCL command.

The hardware monitor controls and monitors hardware components such as modems. Messages (alerts) can be filtered. These messages may be:

- Statistics (traffic information).
- Events (network actions resulting from a failure).
- Alerts.

The session monitor looks after logical aspects of the network. For example, it receives messages each time an LU-LU session is established or terminated. It can also invoke and receive RTM messages from peripheral nodes such as 3174.

NetView's status monitor (STATMON), based on VNCA (VTAM node control application), provides at-a-glance information about the network, including activated and deactivated nodes and the like.

An on-line help facility provided with NetView is meant to not only help operations, but also to aid in the diagnosis of problems.

NetView Graphic Monitor Facility (GMF) can be used with NETCENTER to monitor SNA and non-SNA networks from a single graphic workstation.

Where performance-related network problems occur, they are always particularly hard to track down.

Failures

When the automation software is working well, everyone takes it for granted. The moment it is not completely successful, everyone is after blood. It is essential that after the software is installed and running, people (operators—if any are left—and technical support people) retain a knowledge of how the automation system works, what it is meant to be achieving, and how to fix any problems that occur.

One of the big questions is how does the automation system tell the operators that it has failed? An ideal automation system would know that it had failed and would tell someone.

With NetView Release 1, STATMON can be used for alerting the operators to a problem. With Release 2 the GENALERT gave access to the RECFMS, BASIC, and generic alerts. This greatly improved the interaction with the operator. Alerts can be presented dynamically and are fully supported by "action" and "detail" information.

One way of identifying that the automation has failed is if there is a task supervisor that checks on the automation. Logically, then, it is necessary to have a task manager to ensure that the task supervisor is functioning successfully.

It is possible to have all the individual tasks (AUTOTASKs, CLISTs, timers, and message table-driven events) perform a predetermined task. A consequence of this is that a list of common globals (or control tables) are left behind that can be used as audit trail. At fixed intervals, such as 24 hours or one hour, the common globals could be inspected and incomplete tasks could be identified. These failed tasks could then be recovered.

With NetView Release 2 and above, it is possible to have a small, separate region that would monitor the primary region for failures. If one is unsure as to the reliability of NetView itself, this is not a very practical solution.

Application Recovery

For AOC to recover a failing application or subsystem, a message must be sent. In many instances, applications (like CICS) can be experiencing severe problems without issuing messages to the console. One way of overcoming this problem is to use the NetView Program-to-Program Interface (PPI). The PPI allows application programs to send generic alerts to NetView. This is done by writing an application program that CALLs module CNMNETV. This is illustrated in Fig. 18.5.

To prevent delays, it is a good idea to dedicate initiators to the batch jobs that support the automation.

If a CLIST loops, it will not complete and will probably send multiple identical messages. However, if the CLIST runs under an AUTOTASK there are no outward symptoms of the problem. The AUTOTASK will be in a loop that it cannot break out of to see that the CLIST is in a loop. The machine might possibly come to a halt, remaining permanently in system state. This is very difficult to identify without a good monitor.

Many sites like to be able to turn off automation during the life of a problem. This can be achieved by the use of "switches."

NetView Customization and Maintenance

NetView needs to be customized. It needs to be defined to VTAM as a Communications Network Management (CNM) application. CLISTs or REXX EXECs must be coded. Users' exits are coded for inbound and outbound message routes. These can modify messages going to the log, logging printer, system console, or operator console. Command processors can be customized. These are programs that execute commands from

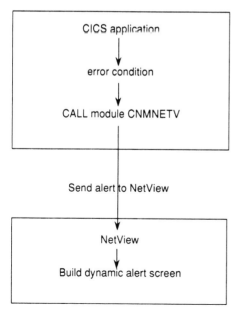

Figure 18.5. Messsage communication.

an operator and carry out particular actions. They have access to Assembler, PL/I, and C programming languages.

Subtasks run under a main task and can be started by a main task. User written subtasks can have a VTAM interface, allowing LU-LU sessions to be established with remote systems. This allows network management facilities to be brought to systems that do not conform to ONM architecture, or systems that only require LU-LU communication with NetView.

Cross Memory Services (XMS) can be used to link to other applications.

Security can also be customized. For example, decisions must be made regarding who is to have log-on authority. Also, there are security considerations regarding the commands that can be issued: for example, which part of the network will they affect, and which operator commands are to be available.

Many problems and pitfalls are likely to beset the person who is responsible for NetView maintenance. For example, the NetView CLIST language has the following unusual characteristics:

- Adequate loop control is lacking.
- There are no procedures.
- The common global variable controls are unusual.

Another problem with CLISTs is that they are interpreted. Any comments in the code [prefixed by an asterisk (*)] will adversely affect the performance of the CLIST—a fact known since NetView Release 1. Any CLISTs without comments are virtually unmaintainable.

The basic CLIST is unable to read or write to datasets. This means that data must be carried in the program material. There are command processors available that allow control tables to be used. To improve performance, a number of these tables are read in at initialization time, and their values are committed to global variables held in storage. CLISTs can access these variables without performing any additional I/Os.

There is a requirement for programmable variables in the message automation table, for example, a common global variable to be part of the IF... THEN processing logic. Conditional testing has to be completed many times within the slow CLIST logic rather than in the faster message table.

Another restriction is that there is no way to override a single entry in a message table. If a single entry is to be replaced, the whole table has to be replaced.

Now that REXX EXECs are available, many of the CLIST limitations can be got round by using REXX.

Flexibility

While the automation process necessarily petrifies certain procedures (for example, if event A occurs, perform action B), it is also necessary for the automation software to have built-in flexibility. This is because it is necessary to plan for the unpredictable.

To facilitate this flexibility, timers should be accessible as switches (common globals) that can be controlled without having to recode the CLIST.

In situations where parameters are held in control files, it is necessary to make the CLIST refresh the value. If the CLIST reads the variable every time it executes, this could double the number of I/Os performed. It is easier to change the value of common global variables that are held in storage than it is to change the control table. This means that the control tables must be read at initialization time, and they must be set up as common globals that can be changed on the fly.

If this kind of advance planning seems impracticable, the alternative is to edit CLISTs on line. Although this provides all the degrees of flexibility that might be required, it falls down in terms of reliability and perhaps defeats the object of the exercise, which is automation.

Associated Software

NetView 2.1 made available the Graphic Monitor Facility (GMF). This allows people with OS/2 Extended Edition Version 1.2 or above to make use of a Graphical User Interface (GUI) to monitor the network. The user of this system can gain a hierarchical view of the network, or they can get a close-up view of a network component, such as NCP type 4 nodes or peripheral node PUs.

The other facility announced with NetView 2.1 was the NetView Bridge Support for Information/Management. Info/Man (Information/Management) is part of Information/Systems from IBM. It can be used for problem management reporting, management of change requests, configuration management, and financial and inventory management. It is used by network operators on a daily basis to track problems and to help them understand the configuration of the network when carrying out problem determination activities.

The most interesting announcement with NetView 2.2 was the LU type 6.2 Transport facility. This uses LU6.2-based sessions to permit NetView applications to interact with remote NetView applications or other applications on suitable devices. Its relevance to automated operations is that it seems to remove the need for NetView/PC.

The recently announced Target System Control Facility (TSCF) automates a number of remote operations functions.

New NetView applications include CICS AO/MVS, and IMS AO/MVS. These facilities are designed to automate start-up, shutdown, and recovery, taking the monotony out of current operations procedures which can involve signing on a great many regions individually. The products are also claimed to be able to identify abnormal failures or abends that are overlooked by traditional performance monitors.

19

Automated Systems Operations and Remote Operations

Remote operations is the process by which one or more mainframes can be controlled from a point that may be at a totally different location from those mainframes. Remote operations covers two different approaches. A computer center may be run by the operators working on a mainframe at a different site, or a mainframe may be controlled by an operator dialing in from a PC who could be located at home. A growing number of companies are running their data centers, which may be physically located at different sites across the country, from a single site.

While it is not essential to automate in order to achieve remote operations, real benefits can be gained only with automation.

Remote operations offers a number of benefits:

- Improved system serviceability.
- Improved system availability.
- Improved system recovery.
- Improved efficiency.
- Reduction in expenditure on operators.
- Staff shortages overcome.
- Flexibility in locating computer center.

The benefits are similar to those for automated operations in general. Improved system recovery can be brought about because the systems programmers could fix problems from home. At night times or on weekends, this is where they will be, and it will save the time spent travelling to a site to fix the problem, if it can be solved from home.

Having a single controlling site means that all the expertise is in one place and the likelihood of finding a solution to a problem is that much greater.

Because staff are not required at the remote site, there will be consequent "bottom line" benefits when it comes to the savings in salaries. This saving can be quite significant if the remote site is located in a part of the country with high living costs and therefore high salaries. There is also no need to spend time trying to recruit staff and train them at these remote sites.

It is possible to put the computer in an unattractive location because remote operations means that people do not need to be at the same location. To maximize cost savings, the hardware should be put where floor space is cheap, and people should be put where people are cheap.

On the down side, it will cost money to move hardware round the country. It will also cost money if people are moved to a new location.

At the depopulated remote site, the lights can be turned out. The physical and environmental security of the site can be better provided. In the event of a fire, appropriate action can be taken immediately and automatically, there is no need to wait for evacuation.

Remote operation is possible nowadays for a number of reasons:

- PCs with 3270 emulation are more reliable.

- Modems (and dial-back security) allow PCs to be put at the end of phone lines.

- Improved cross system communication facilities allow one screen for multi-image networks.

The hardware requirements for remote operations are:

- PCs and 3270 emulation to support the hosts in the network.

- Phone line (dial-up, leased).

- Back-up in case PCs or other devices fail.

- Switching system between main and back-up.

Planning

When a site is thinking about remote operations there are a number of points to consider:

- Concentration of problem management.

- Consolidation of Help Desk services.

- Application of consistent standards.
- Extended working hours because of larger staffing pool.

Concentration of problem management

If all the trained staff are at one location they are more likely to have met a problem before or to be familiar with a suitable method of identifying the source of the problem, and be able to fix it. Also, staffers will be able to learn from each other, which they would not have done if they were isolated in separate locations.

Consolidation of Help Desk services

If all Help Desk services are at one location it is easier to coordinate their activities and ensure that staffers are fully trained to deal with the type of calls they receive.

Application of consistent standards

The procedures that are adopted at the central site can be applied to all the processors that it is controlling. This ensures that no processor is particularly poorly operated, and that all maintain the same high standard.

Extended working hours because of larger staffing pool

It is possible that additional services can be offered because there is a larger pool of operators. This might be longer hours of system availability with operators present, or it might be other opportunities for specialized work (such as special printing that involves different preprinted stationery to be loaded).

Example of Remote Operations

A company may be responsible for two processors locally and five at other locations (see Fig. 19.1). All the computers are controlled from one central location. This location does not necessarily have to be in the same building as the local processors.

The control center would need to run an operator console for each processor and also a system console for each processor. Moving these consoles hundreds of miles can be achieved using, for example, Adacom coax extension boxes or similar.

It is necessary to have the system console in order to perform IPLs on the remote hardware. It is also possible to perform IMLs from this console and a range of diagnostic activities. IBM offers ISCF (Inter System

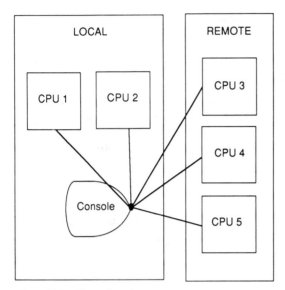

Figure 19.1. Example set-up.

Control Facility) and TSCF (Target System Control Facility), which go
some way toward providing these facilities.

It is possible, with products such as Net/Master (from Systems Center)
to control multiple MVS systems from a single screen image. It uses color
codes to distinguish messages from different systems. This integration is
only possible provided that a degree of message suppression has already
taken place. Net/Master also allows the use of automatic replies and
timer-driven events. This reduces the operators workload even further.

Facilities Management

Facilities management (FM) is a popular concept at the moment. It is a
method adopted by some companies for outsourcing its data processing
requirements. For companies offering facilities management, remote operations is an easy way for them to provide the service. The company
keeps the processor at their site, while the FM providers take the consoles
to their control center.

Remote Operations and NetView

NetView offers remote console operation through the ISCF or TSCF
subtasks. It enables message and command transfer, including remote
IML and IPL. It can be run from a coax-attached PC running ISCF/PC
under PC-DOS.

A focal point is a network node that collects information and makes it available to the network operators. The focal point can be considered to be the hub of the network. It is on one NetView running on one processor and is linked to NetViews running on the remote processors.

ISCF

IBM provides a NetView subtask called Inter System Control Facility (ISCF), which has an interface to VTAM. It is used to send and receive commands, responses, and replies from consoles attached to remote processors. NetView operators can access the operations console as well as the system console at a remote site.

For 3090 sites running MVS/XA or MVS/ESA there is ACA/ISCF (Automated Console Application/Inter System Control Facility). It is comprised of a set of NetView CLISTs, panels, and a command processor.

TSCF

The Target System Control Facility (TSCF) is made from ISCF and ACA. TSCF is designed to allow NetView to control and monitor multiple target systems from a central system.

TSCF runs as a subtask under NetView on the focal point system. It transports messages from the target system to the focal point. Its main use is in initialization and recovery, not in normal running of the target system.

For each remote system a PS/2 workstation is required to be connected to the focal point. The connection can use either a Token Ring LAN or an SNA SDLC line. Before initialization commences, a copy of TSCF software, called the distributed feature, is downloaded to the workstation. The PS/2 acts as a substitute system console and can perform the IML and IPL, set TOD clocks, and so on.

NetView and system start-up

Many sites split NetView into two parts. One part runs in one address space and looks after automation; this part is not dependent on VTAM and may be called the automation NetView. A second NetView address space is used for handling the network; this may be called the network NetView.

It is possible, using NetView on one processor, to IPL a remote processor. IPLs can be performed using ISCF and ACA, or TSCF, running from the NetView focal point. This is illustrated in Fig. 19.2. Following the IPL, ISCF can automate the system until NetView automation is active on the newly IPLed processor.

All the commands used by the focal point NetView are held in common

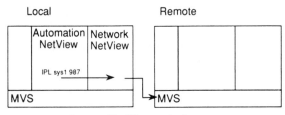

Figure 19.2. Remote NetView control.

global variables. Changes can be made by amending one CLIST. For example, the focal point NetView could issue:

```
IPL sys1 987
```

where 987 is the IPL address for the remote system (sys1). ISCF/ACA will display a confirmation panel that includes:

- Replies to prompts.
- Commands to enter between IPL and NetView initialization.
- The start command for a NetView that looks after automation only.

ISCF IPLs the target system. NetView can be used to respond to start-up messages. The majority of start commands that are to be issued by the system can come from the COMMND*xx* member of PARMLIB. A command in COMMND*xx* can be used to start the automation NetView for that processor.

The automation NetView for the processor can be used to start other system tasks including VTAM. Issuing start commands from NetView is a more flexible approach than issuing them from COMMND*xx*.

Once VTAM is running the automation NetView can start VTAM applications, including a network NetView.

Once VTAM is running on the target system, the focal point NetView operator can start an NNT (NetView-to-NetView) session to the target system. ISCF stops monitoring messages from the target system, and the focal point NetView receives all messages from the target NetView, including alerts.

When the network NetView is initialized on the target system, it can start the network, such as NCPs (network control programs), SNI CDRMs (system network interconnection cross domain resource managers), etc. The majority of the network will, however, be started by ATCCON*xx*.

CLISTs can be run in all NetViews to set timers, which can be used to activate BSC lines and clusters.

Remote Recovery Data Facility

IBM has announced the Remote Recovery Data Facility (RRDF) Version 1 Release 2. This remote site recovery offering provides real-time electronic transmission of log data to an alternative site, providing protection against catastrophic loss. It is available for IMS, CICS, and DB2 environments.

ESCMS

The ESCON Monitor System (ESCMS) can be used by a central site to control devices at a remote site. ESCON Monitor Sensor Adapters can be attached to remote devices and can be used to power those devices on and off.

DFSMSrmm

The Removable Media Manager component of DFSMS/MVS Version 1.1 can be used to control a 3495 tape library dataserver (or ATL). If ESCON channels are used, the 3495 can be located up to 14 miles away from the processor.

20

Automated Systems Operations and SystemView

SystemView was announced by IBM in September 1990 and appears to be an SAA-compliant structure for managing the computing environment. This includes both system management and network management. The systems include IBM systems [e.g., MVS, AIX (Advanced Interactive EXecution), IBM's Unix] and non-IBM ones. The networks include IBM's SNA and non-SNA networks [e.g., OSI (Open System Interconnection), TCP/IP (Transmission Control Program/Internet Protocol), LANs]. Management implies activities such as controlling, configuring, and monitoring. SystemView is not a product that can be purchased, but one step away from being an architecture. It has sometimes been unkindly described as a plan for a plan.

SystemView appears to be a way of simplifying life for the end user such that the processor will automatically perform the activities required by end users without their having to acquire a detailed knowledge of the system and also without involving other MIS personnel. End users should also be able to work from their terminals with data and programs that could be resident on an MVS system, a VM system, or a Unix system without their needing to know that there are any differences among the systems.

SystemView appears to implement the System Management Architecture (SMA), which IBM considers to offer a new way of managing the system so that high-quality service can be provided at a reasonable cost.

System Management Architecture

Many companies cannot afford to invest in people to manage information systems in proportion to the power and number of systems installed. This lack of investment prevents the company from:

- Achieving the high quality of service they want.
- Exploiting new technologies that they cannot manage.

This makes the company less competitive. The shortage of personnel at a company might be because of:

- Lack of skilled staff.
- Insufficient people available in an area.
- Salaries for people in an area too high.
- Demographic shortages of people in the right age group.

System Management Architecture is said to offer the ability to:

- Manage more systems with the existing staff.
- Manage existing systems with fewer staff.
- Obtain greater productivity from the skills of the staff.

System Management involves automation, and other aspects of the data center such as storage management.

SystemView Dimensions

There are three major elements or dimensions to SystemView:

- End user.
- Data.
- Application.

End user dimension

The end user dimension can be thought of as the SAA CUA (common user access) definitions for systems management applications. This means that end users should always have the same interface to the system whether they are working on MVS, VM, or Unix systems. The application that they are working on should "look and feel" the same irrespective of the system or hardware.

Data dimension

The data dimension comprises a relational data model that allows all applications to have a single view of the management information base. This should facilitate data sharing across the various systems management applications. It also reduces the need to keep multiple copies of the same piece of data. The data dimension is SQL-based (structured query language) and appears to use its own repository (not the AD/Cycle repository).

Application dimension

In the application dimension, integration and automation of systems management tasks are meant to be accomplished. This is the dimension that is most relevant in terms of automated operations. The automation will be made possible by the use of program-to-program interfaces.

The application dimension is divided into six disciplines or areas of management:

- *Business management:* Financial administration relating to resources and system operation and planning.

- *Change management:* Planning, scheduling, distribution, control, application, and tracking of hardware, software, and configuration changes required in the system.

- *Configuration management:* The physical and logical connections between resources, as well as the maintenance of the hardware.

- *Operations management:* The use of systems and resources by teleprocessing systems and batch workloads. It will be automated. People considering the move to automated operations need to bear this component in mind when thinking of automated systems operations and SystemView.

- *Performance management:* The collection of performance data for system tuning and capacity planning.

- *Problem management:* The detection, analysis, and control of faults or problems and correcting them.

This new division of labor away from the traditional ones of network, host, storage, database, and administration management is meant to reduce, or remove all together, the duplication of certain tasks and skills at a site. It is therefore suggested that this leads to the best return (in economic terms) and spreads the use of the skills available across all system management tasks.

SystemView Products

Very few products are currently available that fit under the SystemView umbrella. Some of those that are available are:

- SAA Asset Manager/MVS.
- SAA Delivery Manager.
- Application Connection Service.
- Third-party software.

SAA Asset Manager/MVS

SAA Asset Manager/MVS appears to be an implementation of the business management discipline. It seems to offer the ability to collect data on all resources (hardware and software), and to automatically manage the inventory of these resources.

SAA Delivery Manager

SAA Delivery Manager is a centralized software program and file distribution service. It ensures that the correct version of files and software is downloaded from MVS to OS/2, for example. It is described more fully in Chap. 24.

Application Connection Service

Application Connection Service (AConnS) is a necessary prerequisite for SAA Asset Manager/MVS and SAA Delivery Manager. AConnS allows a users with OS/2, or other workstation software, to execute host applications and to treat resources, such as printers, as if they were directly attached.

Third-party software

In June 1991 IBM announced the first of its SystemView partners. These were Bachman Information Systems, Candle Corp., Goal Systems International, and Platinum Technology, Inc. Software supplied by these companies is deemed to be SystemView compatible. In September 1991 IBM announced the IBM International Alliance for SystemView. This partnership includes the original SystemView partners and Information Retrieval Companies (IRC), Inc. In April 1992 Legent took over Goal Systems (finalized in August), and in early July Legent announced its commitment to SystemView by becoming a Development Partner.

Conclusion

SystemView is IBM's way of getting everyone's attention. It promises much, but as yet offers very little. In terms of automated systems operations it is necessary to look at SystemView to see how IBM is planning the future, and then to ensure that the automation fits in with that future. There is no point going for a short-term solution and having to go through the whole painful exercise again in a few years. By the same token it is important to ensure that products look like they will fit into this, and that the supplier of the product can ensure purchasers that they will upgrade their products to fit in with SystemView. In today's environment, System-View can be used to define automated systems operations.

21

Automated Systems Operations and Storage Management

With traditional automated operations, storage management is not a relevant issue because operators do not directly deal with the facilities available with file placement or DASD performance. It is true that operations support, technical support, and systems programmers in the role of data administrator would become involved, but the degree of involvement and the time that the involvement would take place differ from site to site. However, automated system operation does include storage management. The automation of storage management is made possible with IBM's introduction of SMS and the Information Warehouse framework. It is one of the aims of SMS to automate and control data and DASD, and it is clearly IBM's intention to extend the scope of SMS. Therefore, SMS will become an even more important part of automated system operations.

SMS is meant to automate the process of managing space and the placement of datasets. It is necessary because there is an enormous growth in the amount of data stored at a site, and in the number and size of DASD used to store this data.

In addition to SMS looking after end user files, IBM has announced the Information Warehouse framework, which allows users working from terminals or workstations to access data that may be on an IBM mainframe or a connected non-IBM mainframe. End users will have a standard interface with the system no matter where they are working, and will not need to know where the data is located or whether or not the data is in a relational database or not.

DFSMS Background

Data Facility Storage Management Subsystem (DFSMS) is similar to NetView Version 1 in that it is a number of existing products grouped together with a new name. The products that are incorporated into DFSMS are:

- DFP.
- DFDSS.
- DFHSM.
- DFSORT.
- RACF.

The modular nature of DFSMS means that users can order alternative products to the IBM ones, with the exception of DFP.

The May 1992 announcement of DFSMS/MVS Version 1.1 also introduced DFSMSrmm (Removable Media Manager) and DFDSM.

DFP

Data Facility Product (DFP) is itself an agglomeration of earlier products including DFDS (Data Facility Device Support) and DFEF (Data Facility Extended Function). DFDS provided an index to the VTOC (Volume Table of Contents) on a disk. This made accessing a record in a file on disk faster because an entry in the VTOC could be found from the VTOC's index rather than after performing a sequential read of all the VTOC's entries. DFEF introduced a new way of cataloging VSAM files. A new type of catalog, called an ICF (Integrated Catalog Facility), was introduced. This came in two parts: a BCS (basic catalog structure), which contains information about VSAM and non-VSAM datasets, and a VVDS (VSAM volume dataset), which contains information about VSAM datasets only. The BCS is a KSDS; the VVDS is an ESDS. The VVDS must reside on the volume containing the datasets described in it, the BCS can reside anywhere.

DFP is a component of all existing MVS operating systems, and is required to perform I/O and data management services for users. With MVS/ESA, DFP supports dataspaces and hyperspaces.

With DFSMS/MVS Version 1.1 the product is being written as DFSMSdfp.

DFDSS

Data Facility DataSet Services is primarily a back-up and restore product. It is the product used to ensure that SMS datasets are copied (usually to tape) so that they can be restored should the original dataset be deleted or become corrupted for any reason.

DFDSS can also be used for disk space management. If a disk pack is frequently used for files that are created and soon deleted, the space available for files will become fragmented. This will have performance consequences because accessing a file will take longer because the read/write heads on the disk will have to move to more than one location to read in the data. It is possible with DFDSS to DEFRAG (defragment) a disk. Once all the files are copied to tape, they can be reloaded to the disk contiguously. In this way, all the free space can be in one area. Therefore the access times for new and existing files will be fast.

A popular alternative to DFDSS is FDR/ABR/CPK from Innovation Data Processing.

Part of DFDSS is DFDSS/ISMF, the Interactive Storage Management Facility. This is an interface to DFDSS and SMS that can be used by human storage administrators. ISMF is an ISPF (Interactive System Productivity Facility) application. ISMF can be used to specify data classes, storage classes, management classes, and storage groups to SMS.

With DFSMS/MVS Version 1.1 the product is being written as DFSMSdss.

Back-up problems.   As the amount of data stored at a site increases, the time available for back-ups is shrinking to nil at some sites. If incremental back-ups are used extensively, recovery time increases dramatically. While the recovery is going on, work waiting to be performed is building up. One way of getting round this is to use ABARS (Aggregate Back-up and Recovery System) available with DFHSM Version 2.5. This allows individual applications to be recovered while work is being performed. On the down side, it takes more time for all files to be backed up each time.

With the growth in LAN systems it is important to back up data across LAN systems, i.e., from PCs and workstations. This saves the workstation user having to remember to do it, and ensures that the data is managed properly. However, this introduces extra problems in terms of performing back-ups.

DFHSM

Data Facility Hierarchical Storage Manager (DFHSM) is designed to handle data migration and recall. At any site, data can be loaded from some devices into storage faster than from other devices. For example, disks allow faster I/O than tapes. It is better, in terms of performance, if datasets that are frequently used are stored on faster devices than those that are infrequently used. DFHSM will migrate datasets that are not regularly accessed from high-speed devices to slower-speed devices. It will also keep a record of where the dataset is located so that it can be quickly recalled if a user requires it.

A popular alternative to DFHSM is DMS/OS from Sterling Software. With DFSMS/MVS Version 1.1 the product is being written as DFSMShsm.

DFSORT

Data Facility SORT is IBM's sort utility. It makes use of hiperspace to speed up sorting activities, but is generally considered to be inferior to third-party sort utility packages. Its inclusion in SMS seems a small aberration because none of the other IBM utility programs are, such as IEB or IEH utilities. Some people have suggested unkindly that its inclusion is a marketing ploy.

RACF

Resource Access Control Facility (RACF) is an access control product. In order for a resource (user-id, file, etc.) to be protected it must be explicitly defined as an RACF resource. Using RACF replaces the need for a SYS1.UADS file for TSO user-ids.

RACF is included as part of SMS because it ensures that only authorized users can access the system, and more importantly for SMS it restricts access to data to authorized users. In terms of security, this prevents data being available to others and also prevents others altering or corrupting the data.

RACF is unusual insofar as it is the only product included in DFSMS that does not begin DF. Clearly the marketing people slipped up.

Popular alternatives to RACF are listed in Appendix B.

DFSMSrmm

With DFSMS/MVS Version 1.1 came the introduction of the 3495 tape library dataserver and the Removable Media Manager (RMM). The 3495 is IBM's ATL, and is based on 3490 cartridge tape drives. Cartridge tapes are selected and loaded. Controlling what gets written to a tape and how much of the tape is used is RMM. At a typical site, only a small part of each tape is ever used, RMM makes better use of this unused tape capacity and thereby reduces the number of tapes required.

DFDSM

Data Facility Distributed Storage Manager is IBM's client-server system that allows storage management and data access services in a multivendor network environment. DFDSM allows MVS (and VM) systems to act as back-up and archive servers for LAN file servers and workstations (including DOS, Windows, AIX/6000, OS/2, and NetWare). The back-up and other functions will take place automatically under the control of the mainframe-based software.

What Is SMS?

The concept behind System Managed Storage is that humans are fallible, and that the best way of doing a job right every time is to automate it. SMS lets the computer system manage data storage rather than the human JCL writer, or the human data administrator, or any other human. In fact, the system is meant to control the storage, accessibility, retrieval, and archiving of data.

SMS has been talked about, in one form or another, by IBM for many years. However, only in the recent past has something been available to manifest the aims of SMS.

As far as end users are concerned, their data must be available to them whenever and wherever they want it. It must also be immediately available to them and not available to anyone else. SMS is meant to ensure that these requirements are met. It is also meant to ensure that the requirements are met better than they would be on a system without SMS.

Benefits of SMS

A number of benefits are associated with the use of SMS. Many of these benefits are the same as any given for automated systems operations, such as improved service for users, fewer mistakes made by humans, and fewer humans required.

Other benefits that have been associated with SMS are:

- Increased productivity of storage management staff.
- Reduced manpower requirements.
- Minimized costs.
- Improvements in responsiveness.
- Improved service with increased productivity of application developers.
- Maximized performance for users.
- Improvements in satisfaction.
- Improvements in efficiency.
- Increased DASD space utilization.
- Optimized free space usage.
- Improved device efficiency because system selects optimum blocksizes for devices.

- More efficiently used storage media. (This therefore reduces the amount of increase in storage media required by a site and consequently saves money. It will not require more storage administrators even though more data is stored, thus saving money.)

- Ability to manage more disk storage.

- Large reduction in number of tape mounts.

- Ability to adopt specific management policies for data storage rather than having to manage data storage with JCL.

- Effective control of disk usage from a central point.

- Ability to impose site standards and policies.

- Preservation of information safety.

- Removal of unneeded on-line data.

- Easier administration of users.

- Reduced training needs.

- Insulation of end users from physical hardware characteristics.

- Fewer mistakes with less JCL to write.

- Reduction in required skill level to perform successfully.

- Simplified user interfaces for allocating and maintaining data.

- Separation of a user's logical view of data from the actual physical device characteristics.

- Creation of VSAM clusters from JCL statements, eliminating IDCAMS.

- Ability to allocate temporary VSAM datasets.

SMS Objectives

SMS has four main objectives. These are:

- *Security:* Secure data, back-up/recovery, interface to access control.

- *Dataset management:* Allocation and control of datasets.

- *Space management:* Maximizing available free space.

- *Reporting:* Providing information about the contents and use of storage.

DFSMS

When SMS goes live, it runs in its own address space, not as part of the Master scheduler address space or in an initiator address space.
   DFSMS makes use of four constructs:

- Data classes.
- Management classes.
- Storage classes.
- Storage groups.

An installation needs many sets of these constructs, each identified by a unique name. These rules are implemented by a set of programs known as automatic class selection (ACS) routines.

Data classes

Data classes can be used so that JCL writers do not need to code DCB information when allocating a dataset. Dataset attributes are predefined in the SMS data class name. A user does not even have to specify a data class name if automatic class selection (ACS) routines are coded. ACS can select a data class based on a dataset name. In order for ACS to become a working part of automated systems operations, it is necessary to standardize dataset names at a site. This is a formidable challenge.

Data class is used to define sets of default space allocation values and DCBs for datasets to be allocated.

A data class definition contains standard dataset allocation information for specific types of datasets. A type of dataset may be determined by the last qualifier of a dataset name, such as CNTL, LIST, and so on.

Management classes

Management classes are used to define migration and recovery characteristics. These characteristics can be specified by dataset or by volume.

Management class sets back-up and archiving requirements for a dataset. They specify the frequency with which datasets are to be backed up or migrated, and the length of time that they are to be maintained on DASD.

Storage classes

Storage classes specify the response time requirements of a dataset, i.e., milliseconds of response time per I/O. SMS will attempt to meet the specified criteria. There is a guaranteed space option, which when invoked means that no attempt is made to meet time objectives. The guaranteed space option is used mainly to preallocate a multivolume dataset.

If guaranteed space has not been requested, SMS will locate up to 15 storage groups, that the dataset can access, that have enough space for the primary allocation. A storage group defines a group of volumes. Storage group selection depends on whether the storage class has a read or write bias that makes it eligible for cache access.

If there is no acceptable storage available—i.e., with the necessary response time objectives—SMS will allocate the file on the first device that can satisfy the primary allocation space requirements.

Storage groups

Storage groups manage space for storage classes. They can also include attributes for migration and recovery. Defining the correct volume mix for each storage group requires a full knowledge of the system's workload and its potential growth. There is no automation of this process.

Storage groups are used to group the physical disk volumes into logical disk pools, and to define volume-related dump and archival criteria.

When new disks are installed, JCL does not have to be changed to include them, they can be simply added to a storage group to become usable.

Automatic class selection

The ACS (automatic class selection) routines are invoked whenever a new dataset is created. They are used to determine which rules to apply to the new dataset. The appropriate construct names are passed to DFP in order to decide how much space is required, and which volume to place the dataset on. This automation controls the allocation of datasets. Figure 21.1 illustrates the techniques for achieving storage management goals.

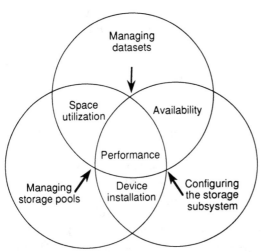

Figure 21.1. Techniques for achieving storage management goals.

SMS Costs

The costs involved with SMS are:

- *Time and effort to set up the SMS system:* A few storage classes, a few management classes, and a few storage groups are required. A large number of data classes must be specified to allow for all dataset sizes and other characteristics, such as sequential file and the like.

- *Disk space:* To store control files and construct files (source and live versions disk space is needed). In multi-CPU environments a communication dataset (COMMDS) is used. Catalogs will be larger to store information for all datasets and extra space for GDG ROLLIN/ROLL-OUT activity.

- *CPU cycles:* These are consumed by ACS routines and processing constructs when datasets are created, and to support a new field in the VVDS.

- *Training someone to write ACS routines.*

- *Software:* MVS/SP Version 3 or 4; DFP Version 3; DFHSM, DFDSS, DFSORT, RACF, DFSMSrmm, DFDSM or a third-party equivalent of them.

SMS Hardware Requirements

At the time of writing, to fully implement SMS it is necessary to have:

- A processor that can run MVS/ESA.
- Expanded storage.
- 3390 Model 3 DASD controllers.

The Information Warehouse Framework

Among IBM's September 1991 announcements was the Information Warehouse framework. This framework is designed to make the life of the end user much simpler by allowing activities to happen transparently that previously would have required a great deal of activity by programmers and the MIS department. End users are able to access data from a wide variety of databases and from both IBM and non-IBM platforms. This is illustrated in Fig. 21.2.

The Information Warehouse framework is composed of three parts: These are:

- The enterprise data element.
- The data delivery element.
- The applications and decision support systems.

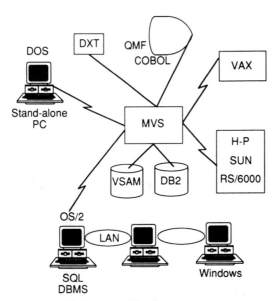

Figure 21.2. Information Warehouse.

The enterprise data element

The enterprise data element, at the center of the Information Warehouse, consists of fully functioned database management systems that provide data integrity, security, recovery, reliability, availability, and performance.

The enterprise data element makes use of Enterprise Data Access/SQL (EDA/SQL) from Information Builders. This is a family of four client-server products that support servers, communication links, data access drivers, and other tools. It allows end users from terminals or PCs to access data on an IBM mainframe or a DEC minicomputer without needing to know what is going on. The four products are:

- EDA/SQL Server, a host component that processes SQL requests against relational and nonrelational data.
- API/SQL (Application Programming Interface/SQL), a call level API.
- EDI/Link, a modular system of communication interfaces.
- EDA/Extender Products, direct interfaces from popular SQL-based tools.

The data delivery element

The data delivery element is the means by which the right data is supplied to an application user. The data can come from any local or remote database system supporting DRDA (distributed relational database architecture).

The data delivery element makes use of DRDA. It is an architecture that provides connectivity between applications and a relational database management system. It supports SQL as the standardized interface that applications use to access distributed relational data. SQL can now be used to access nonrelational data (an estimated 90 percent) of the data at a site.

The application and decision support systems

The decision support part of Information Warehouse includes IBM's QMF (Query Management Facility) and DXT (Data eXTract) among other products. SAS Institute's SAS system, for example, supports the Information Warehouse. SAS is a decision support system used at many MVS sites.

Optimizing File Performance

All MVS sites make use of VSAM (virtual storage access method) datasets. If care is not taken, it is quite possible for the datasets to grow very large, and for the time taken to retrieve a record from within a dataset to be large. Traditionally, it is the programmers responsibility to look at the output from an IDCAMS LISTCAT and decide on the optimum values to use when defining a VSAM dataset. With a large number of VSAM datasets it is physically impossible to check every day to optimize the datasets. It is possible, using various combinations of software [for example, FAVER and VSAMAID from Goal Systems (now Legent)] to automate the process. VSAM files can be backed up to tape, the optimum values for the files can be calculated by the software, and the data can be reloaded into the optimized datasets. The activity can take place automatically, and can be started at a particular time each day by the automation software. The benefit to the end user of doing this is that record retrieval times are always the fastest possible. This makes the end user and thereby the company more productive.

Boole & Babbage's product called DASD ADVISOR can be used to identify performance problems on DASD. It is an expert system that analyzes performance data to identify the causes of the performance problems. It also recommends corrective action. At most sites where the product is used, the recommendations are carried out by humans. It would be possible to automate this activity.

22

Automated Systems Operations and Expert Systems

Much of the automation that can be performed at a site is fairly straightforward and can be done using the tools that are already available. However, if a site is trying to automate all the activities performed currently by operators, they will reach that last 5 percent of messages that are not always answered in the same way and cannot be answered simply by asking the system one or two straightforward questions. They will, therefore, be unable to push their automation activity any further. This is where expert systems can be used.

Many third-party automation products make use of expert systems as a way of making a more effective product. The software is either given, or creates, a model of what constitutes the optimum system and then operates in such a way as to try to achieve the optimum. Products such as storage management software work in this way.

Expert systems are programs that reproduce human decision making from a set of precoded rules. They are an attempt to capture human expertise and to use that expertise within a limited framework. They are considered within automated system operation because, when properly used, they can always perform as well as the best operator at a site.

If, for example, a line was to fail, the expert system could schedule recovery actions for that resource. It could then test to ensure that the recovery was satisfactory. If the component failed repeatedly, it could reroute traffic and schedule the component to be repaired.

Expert System Structure

Expert systems are a product of artificial intelligence (AI) research. Expert systems have two distinct parts:

- The inference engine.
- The rule base.

The inference engine

The inference engine is a program that controls the flow of logic. With expert systems, the flow is not necessarily linear and predetermined. The logic is recursive. The inference engine reads through the rule base repetitively and follows a different path each time. Almost all the data will have an effect on the path taken. This means that most expert systems have a very large number of combinations of rules and data. Inference engines do either forward chaining or backward chaining.

Forward chaining. Forward chaining means that the expert system begins with information and moves from rule to rule, testing whether known facts satisfy the condition statements. When they do, the rule is actioned.

Backward chaining. Backward chaining means that the expert system begins by looking for a particular goal or conclusion. It moves from rule to rule asking for information to see whether all the condition statements can be satisfied and the goal reached.

The rule base

An expert system's rule base is a set of "if... then..." statements. These represent the expertise that the system is trying to emulate. Some expert systems use only natural language (such as English) sentences to test whether a statement is true or false.

Expert System Benefits

The benefits of using an expert system are many:

- Service is improved.
- Expertise is preserved within a company.
- Decision making is sped up.
- All decisions are consistent.
- Redundant training is reduced.
- On-site experts are able to spend their time more productively.
- Expenditure is saved.

Many automated systems operations products make use of expert systems, such as DASD Advisor from Boole & Babbage.

YES/MVS

IBM's first attempt at an expert system for MVS was Yorktown Expert System/MVS (YES/MVS). The product was considered to be clumsy and somewhat profligate in terms of machine resources. It also required VM to be running with MVS running under it.

YES/MVS made use of three virtual machines running under VM. The first virtual machine contained the expert system. This had been developed using the language OPS5 at Carnegie-Mellon University. The second virtual machine ran an MVS Communication Control Facility (MCCF). MCCF was written in REXX and Assembler, and allowed the expert system and MVS to communicate. The third virtual machine was responsible for the expert system/operator interface.

YES/MVS provided nine operational functions:

- Quiesce and IPL activity.
- Software subsystem monitoring and restarting.
- Performance monitoring.
- Large batch jobs scheduling.
- JES queue space management.
- SMF management.
- Corrective action for MVS-detected hardware errors.
- Corrective action for problems in channel-to-channel transmission.
- Incident reporting.

OPC/A

IBM also produced Operations Planning and Control/Advanced (OPC/A). This suite of programs was meant to aid planning, controlling, and automating batch production work. Its main claim for inclusion in this chapter is that it was a forerunner to OPC/ESA.

OPC/ESA

Operations Planning and Control/Enterprise Systems Architecture (OPC/ESA) is a combination of the function of OPC/A and the concepts behind YES/MVS. OPC/ESA provides production batch workload scheduling management. It also provides a restart mechanism on a stand-by system in a sysplex that is running OPC/ESA. During recovery it transfers processing work from the failing processor.

OPC/ESA is made up of two components plus a user interface. All OPC/ESA installations must have the Tracker function, which monitors events on its host processor. One processor in a sysplex, or single processor complex, must have the Controller function. This provides:

- Event status query facilities.

- Control specifications, using fill-in-the-blanks dialogs.

- Operator on-line work list generation.

- Exits for customization.

- Interface to SystemView and other products, such as RACF.

TIRS

The Integrated Reasoning Shell (TIRS) is an expert system that runs under OS/2, AIX, and VM, as well as MVS. Users are meant to develop applications under OS/2. They are next meant to generate an Export Language version of it. The Export Language version is transferred to MVS, compiled, and run.

SAA SystemView Automated Operations Expert/MVS (AOEXPERT/ MVS) uses artificial intelligence techniques embedded in The Integrated Reasoning Shell to provide a realtime decision making facility for advanced automation.

AOEXPERT/MVS

In September 1991 IBM announced SAA SystemView Automated Operations Expert/MVS (AOEXPERT/MVS). It is meant to reduce system outages and the impact of problems, thus improving system availability and the productivity of the MIS department. AOEXPERT provides automation facilities to manage system problems according to customer policy. Its capabilities include outage avoidance for excessive resource utilization by JES2 and console message streaming, and it can be extended through customer-developed routines.

AOEXPERT/MVS is integrated with AOC/MVS and NetView for MVS and provides a SystemView-conforming end user interface. It uses the artificial intelligence techniques of TIRS for System/370 to provide an advanced real-time decision making facility. "It is an important step towards the implementation of systems that will manage themselves, a key element of the SystemView direction," according to IBM.

23

Automated Systems Operations and the Help Desk

Because the number of computers in use is rising, and because more end users are making use of the services offered by the computers, more problems are being experienced by people, and the people need somewhere to turn to for help with the problems. In the past, end users have asked each other for help—with varying degrees of success—or they have phoned the operators. Operators would check the system, the line, and anything else necessary in order to solve the users' problems. Although the operators had access to the consoles and could check information quickly and make changes easily, they were also very busy, and were not famous for their "bedside manner" when dealing with users.

Many sites decided to set up a Help Desk. The role of the Help Desk was to take the calls from users and prevent the operators from being continuously disturbed. With the move to automated system operations, where there may not be any operators to take calls, the Help Desk becomes even more important. It should be remembered that users come to the Help Desk not just with problems, but also with straightforward inquiries. One other important factor in the growth of Help Desks is that IBM has been promoting the concept. The logical flow of communications to a Help Desk is illustrated in Fig. 23.1.

The Help Desk is promoted as a central point of contact for users when they experience any kind of problem. The Help Desk operatives may be able to solve the problem immediately, or they may have to pass on (escalate) the problem for someone else to solve. That "someone else" may be an operator or technical specialist.

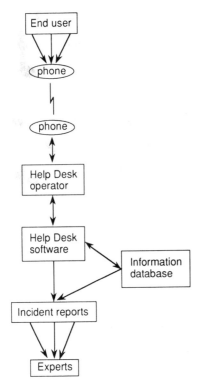

Figure 23.1. Help Desk logical communications flow.

A Help Desk is needed at a site because of the growth in end user computing and the need to support complex systems and software packages bought from a number of different vendors.

Benefits

The suggested benefits from operating a Help Desk are:

- The level of service offered to end users is enhanced.
- Trivial problems can be solved immediately.
- Complex problems can be escalated to the correct person for solution.
- Operators (where they exist) are not constantly interrupted.
- End users need only know one phone number to use when they need help, instead of the numbers for many departments.
- Users queries can be dealt with in a prompt and professional manner.
- End user perception of the MIS department is improved.
- The collection of statistics allow the quality and reliability of various

hardware and software components of the system to be monitored. When appropriate, action can be taken, such as to change the component, supplier, or other aspect of the system.

- It is easier to keep track of a problem and find out how long it took to be resolved.

- The overall performance of the company is enhanced.

- It is easier to ensure that SLAs are being met.

- There is improved financial control.

- Security is improved because access to certain files and facilities is restricted to Help Desk staff.

Help Desk Automation Software

Automation of the Help Desk ranges from data entry on a PC, a front end for the problem management system, to on-line help facilities and problem determination aids, and the use of expert systems to provide support facilities for the Help Desk analysts.

There is a variety of problem logging software available for Help Desks. Some is mainframe based, and some is PC based. An example of mainframe software is Info/Man (Information Management System) from IBM, CA-Netman from Computer Associates, and PNMS III from Peregrine Systems. On the PC side are products such as IBM's Problem Management Productivity Services (PMPS) and Help Desk Expert Automation Tool (HEAT) from Bendata Management Systems. These last two products incorporate expert system capabilities, and can be used to train newer Help Desk staff in the problem determination process. For more experienced staff, the software can be used to speed up the process of problem solving.

Magic Solutions offers Help Desk and asset management software called Support Magic. This provides inventory tracking, configuration management, problem tracking, and management reporting.

AICorp supplies First Class, an expert system for Help Desks. It makes use of menus, forms, hypertext, and hypergraphics.

Help Desk Operation

The Help Desk can be set up with highly trained, highly motivated operatives who have access to all consoles and can make changes to the way the system is running and to the network. The Help Desk operatives can have access to diagnostic tools and may be able to resolve the majority of user calls. This is what is called an "intelligent" Help Desk. It is possible to set up a Help Desk whose sole function is to receive calls, log the problem, and pass the questions and problems received onto someone else for solution. This is an "unintelligent" Help Desk. Most Help Desks fall somewhere in between these extremes.

In a recent survey (*The IBEX Bulletin,* December 1991), it was found that 80 percent of MVS/ESA sites now have a Help Desk.

For a Help Desk to run successfully, thought must be given to the following areas:

- Terms of reference.
- Management of the Help Desk.
- Targets and objectives of the Help Desk.
- Service level management.
- Monitoring.

The *terms of reference* of the Help Desk should include:

- Availability.
- Problem solving.
- Call logging.
- Problem control.
- Priorities.
- Call handling.
- Attitude.

The *management* of a Help Desk will include:

- Staffing.
- Training.
- Targets and objectives.
- Service level management.
- Problem and change.
- Installation management.
- Monitoring.
- Help Desk tools.

The Help Desk must be set *targets and objectives,* including:

The IBEX Bulletin is a monthly survey of IBM mainframe and compatible sites throughout the world. It is published by Xephon plc.

- Meeting terms of reference.
- Measuring overall performance.
- Measuring individuals performance.
- Not accepting failures.
- Setting performance targets.
- Setting future targets.
- Producing a monthly brochure.
- Holding performance meetings.
- Meeting other IS department heads.
- Identifying trends and peaks.

Service level management of the Help Desk is important and must cover the following areas:

- Service must depend on Help Desk.
- Staff must understand service levels.
- Service levels must be measured.
- Failures must be highlighted.
- Mean time statistics are vital.
- Vendor management is critical.

Monitoring of Help Desk must include the following requirements:

- All calls must be logged.
- Data must be analyzed weekly.
- Trends must be highlighted.
- Terms of reference must be highlighted.
- Staff performance must be monitored.
- Monitoring and analysis will reduce costs.

For a successful Help Desk, managers need:

- Terms of reference.
- Discipline.
- Imagination.
- Business objectives.
- Initiative.
- Correct tools.

- Staff policies.
- A clear strategy.

If the Help Desk does not work successfully, users' perceptions of the MIS department will deteriorate, and all the benefits and improvements in service brought about by the introduction of automated systems operations will not be appreciated.

Help Desk Development

When setting up a Help Desk, the best policy is to ensure that all relevant departments are consulted from the beginning. This is because no two Help Desks are identical, and it is important to ensure that the Help Desk at a site is tailored to exactly meet the requirements of that site. In practice, representatives from end user departments, operations, network operations, system programmers, application programmers, and management should be consulted. It is at this stage that the sort of problems to be solved by the Help Desk should be decided, and also the person to whom Help Desk staff will report should be chosen.

The Help Desk budget will have to be decided on. This decision will have an effect on all further decisions. The more money that is available, the wider is the choice of hardware and software for the Help Desk. Also, the budget will affect the number of Help Desk operatives and their quality. Is the cost to be taken from a particular department's annual budget, or is the company going to allocate extra money for the Help Desk? Who is to control spending this money?

Other areas associated with the Help Desk that should be decided include:

- The level of intelligence of the Help Desk.
- The status of the Help Desk.
- When services are to be available.
- The number of staff.
- The procedures to follow.
- Hardware and software requirements.

The level of intelligence of the Help Desk

"Intelligent" Help Desks are staffed by people who can solve many user problems immediately. "Unintelligent" Help Desks act simply as a focal point for calls from users; calls are logged and passed on to the appropriate personnel for resolution.

The status of the Help Desk

It must be decided whether the Help Desk is to be an autonomous department manned by its own trained staff, or an adjunct to operations, manned by the remaining operators who may have other duties to perform at the same time.

When services are to be available

It must be decided whether the Help Desk is to be available between 9 A.M. and 5 P.M. only (the core working day) or whenever computer services are available. With the growth of international links, users in one part of the world could be experiencing problems during their 9-to-5 working day, while the host mainframe Help Desk staff are at home asleep. It must also be decided whether to work five days a week or seven.

The number of staff

Assuming that the Help Desk is to be manned by its own staff (rather than by operators), decisions must be made as to how many staffers to employ. Staff numbers must be high enough to be able to answer user queries within an acceptable time frame. There must also be enough staff to cover for holidays and illness. If more than one shift is to be worked, enough staff to cover both shifts must be employed.

It must also be decided what specialist staffers are to be employed. Are highly technical staff required? Are staff with foreign language skills required?

The procedures to follow

Once the role of the Help Desk is established, and the number and level of personnel to run it are selected, the procedures to be adopted must be decided. These procedures must be clearly laid down so that everyone knows what to do in all foreseen situations, and the procedures must all be tested to ensure that they work. If they do not, they must be modified, and all documentation updated. Procedures should include everything from how to answer the phone to when to escalate a problem.

Hardware and software requirements

It must be decided what hardware and software are required for the Help Desk—telephones, pads, PCs, etc. It is important to try out anything that is to be purchased so that the best alternative is selected.

24

Automated Systems Operations, Service Level Agreements, and Asset Management

At any site, the MIS department should be thought of as offering a service to customers, i.e., the other departments within the company. For that service to be satisfactory to the end users (the customers) it is important that a level of service is agreed and maintained, and also that the MIS department knows what hardware and software the end users are using. It may be possible to improve the service offered by simply upgrading a piece of hardware at the user's end. Agreements between the MIS department and user departments are usually referred to as *service level agreements* (SLAs). Control of what the end user is using can be called *asset management*.

The introduction of automated systems operations is usually associated with an improvement in the service that the MIS department makes to the end users. This can not only be reflected in new SLAs, but also the news of the improved service should be made known to everyone.

In terms of asset management, automated systems operations means that control of the hardware and software in use will have to be automated. This should result in the usual improvements in service and performance.

Service Level Agreements

The objective of SLAs is to ensure mutual understanding between customers (users) and the MIS department regarding the services provided, the resources required, and the costs involved.

SLAs can cover any of the following:

- MIS services.
- Remote terminal support.
- New developments that may be necessary.

An SLA should specify the parameters under which an application or service is to be delivered to the end user. Typically, an SLA document should include the following areas:

- Service definition.
- Scope.
- Availability.
- Response time.
- Support.
- Limitations.
- Other.

It is usual for any agreement between the MIS department and any other department within the company to be made up of a number of subagreements.

SLAs are fundamental to the success of a company, and senior management should be involved both in agreeing that an SLA is at the right level of service and in investigating why an SLA is being broken, if it is. It should be regarded as part of the business plan of the company that the level of service offered by one department to another is at a sufficiently high level for that company to be commercially successful. Senior management involvement with SLAs should send the message to everyone in the company that everyone and every department is working towards a common goal.

If SLAs are not implemented, no one really knows the level of the service delivered. MIS managers may consider the service good enough, users may not. The SLA gives them a chance to agree on a value. Without SLAs, end users' expectations of service may be totally unrealistic. The SLA offers an opportunity to make that expectation reasonable. It also makes the MIS's expectations reasonable. If applications are implemented, and response times drop, but no one complains, MIS managers may think the service is still fine.

SLAs that work should be agreed between the departments involved. They should not be imposed from outside. The SLAs should reflect the business environment. If end users are expecting a 24-hour service, the MIS department will have to arrange for someone to be available 24 hours a day. Effective SLAs must be financially realistic. If end users demand 100 percent availability, then the costs involved in offering that level of availability must be examined. It may be more cost effective to offer 95 percent or 98 percent availability. SLAs should reflect the common goals of the company. SLAs should contain some form of accountability. If the service were offered to an outside company, financial penalties could be imposed. Internal SLA must offer some accountability if the service drops, and also senior management must become involved in finding out what is required to restore the level of service, work out the costs of that restoration, and decide whether it is in the company's interest to restore the service level or agree on a new SLA.

For SLAs to work they must be constantly monitored and managed to succeed. No SLA should ever be changed without the agreement of all parties concerned.

The SLA should be in effect for a definite time period, such as one year, then renegotiated if necessary in the light of experience and new business needs.

To help with SLAs, IBM has Service Level Reporter (SLR). Many sites prefer third-party products such as SAS (from the SAS Institute) or MICS (from Legent). SLR is SystemView compliant. It can be used to report on:

- MVS/ESA.
- CICS/ESA.
- IMS fast path.
- RACF.
- SMS and non-SMS storage.

When MIS department members are thinking about the level of service that they can offer, they should look at things from end users' point of view. End users know only that their system is down if they get no response from the terminal. They do not know, or care, which part in the chain between the terminal and the application within the processor is broken. Therefore, as far as availability is concerned, it is necessary to have all components available, not just the processor for 99 percent (or however much) of the time. For end users, the most important thing is service, which is usually associated with response times in their minds.

The introduction of automated systems operations is an opportunity to renegotiate the service levels to be offered to the end users, and they should in most cases result in the improved level of service available being reflected in the new SLA.

Asset Management

Asset management is the modern jargon for what used to be called (and in many places, including within the SystemView application dimension, still is) problem and change management. Asset management covers such areas as:

- Control program source.
- Production JCL.
- File definition parameters.
- Report distribution.

It is worth remembering that the assets of a company include the information produced, as well as the hardware, software, and people. The value of the information produced to a company is therefore very high although difficult to quantify.

With the introduction and extension of automation, asset management becomes easier because fewer manual tasks are being performed.

What is needed for asset management is a software tool that can control problems and the distribution of changes.

For tracking and coordinating changes to the system environment IBM offers SMP/E (System Modification Program/Extended). SMP/E manages to report on changes to the environment and control the implementation of those changes. Unfortunately, many users consider the product to be unsuitable for use outside the system environment. The reasons given usually include system complexity and overhead.

The change management aspect of asset management will detect, track, and report on change events and activities.

Software changes may be made to code and the location of the code may change, for example, during development or when emergency fixes are applied; and special exception changes may be made to code that is sent to one of a company's satellite data centers. These program variations can impact on the complex web of other programs wrapped around them. These minor variations in code and location highlight the importance of good asset management.

Asset management means more than just documenting problems, changes, and configuration in a nonintegrated repository. Problem, change, and configuration management must all interact. If a problem occurs, a change to the configuration of the system may resolve it.

In terms of automation, it is not enough for the preautomation pieces of paper to go on line. The system must be rethought and then automated. This involves:

- Automatic solution of problems.

- Unresolved problems must be automatically tracked.

- The severity of unresolved problems must automatically be escalated over time.

In addition to the mainframe hardware and software, as more and more PCs become connected on LANs, it is important to know exactly what a site has in terms of PC or workstation hardware and software.

The distribution and installation of PC-based software for cooperative processing applications often need to be synchronized with the installation of MVS-based software with which it must interact.

Going from desk to desk, manually writing down what each person has in terms of hardware and software, is not a viable choice at almost all sites. An automation package is clearly required.

In addition to knowing the name of a product installed, version control is very important. As well as its importance for auditing, it is important when upgrading and ensuring that pirate software is not in use. It also makes training easier if it is known which software people are likely to use.

Automated recoverability of software on remote nodes in order to maintain consistency with host software versions is also necessary.

Additionally, automated software installation needs to be supported during off hours at unattended sites. This minimizes the disruption to business activity. IBM offer DCMF/MVS (Distributed Change Management Facility) to do this.

Inventory control will issue an alert if a device is stolen, and identify unused or seldom used devices. It will also spot which component fails most frequently, and help identify what needs upgrading.

For PCs that are not connected to a mainframe, a number of packages are available for inventory control. These are listed in Appendix B.

SAA Asset Manager

SAA Asset Manager is IBM's SystemView-blessed asset management software. Its job is basically to keep a record of what hardware and software a site possesses. SAA Asset Manager provides the following application functions:

- Inventory management.

- Resource life cycle tracking, allocation and return, accounting data and maintenance functions.

- Order processing.

- Invoice processing.
- Reconciliation of invoices against orders and leases.
- Synchronization of inventory record handling with order tracking.
- Service request handling.
- Definition of required activities, conditions, required actions, staff allocation, and worklist management.

SAA Delivery Manager

SAA Delivery Manager allows software and data to be delivered to networked OS/2 workstations from an MVS host. It is a SystemView product. It is very useful in asset management in ensuring that all networked OS/2s are using the same product and the same release of a product.

25

Automated Systems Operations and Automation Audits

An *audit* usually consists of a detailed examination of the accounts of a company to ensure that they are in order. In terms of automated systems operations, it is an opportunity to examine the way that activities are carried out by a company, and, using this as a basis, areas that could benefit from automation can be identified and examined more closely.

The areas that are usually considered first are those associated with automating the work of the operator, including:

- Suppressing messages.
- Replying to messages.
- Issuing commands.
- Scheduling.
- Report distribution.
- Tape handling.
- Disk housekeeping.

The results of the audit will indicate which areas can benefit from automation, and also what priorities can be assigned to each area.

The audit also provides information to help in the planning process. It can help when deciding time scales for the implementation of the automation.

Conducting an Audit

Before the audit begins it is necessary to decide:

- How long the audit will take.
- Who is going to conduct it.
- What procedure is to be adopted.
- What areas are to be audited.

How long the audit will take

If the time allocated for the audit is too short, important areas may be missed out. If the time allocated is too long, the original objectives will perhaps be lost.

Who is going to conduct it

Typically the best people to include in the team of auditors are people who understand the procedures under examination. This means that the team will comprise mainly people with an operations background. The number of people required will very much depend on the site conducting the audit.

The best person to head the team might at first seem to be the operations manager or the data center manager. However, it is unlikely that they can be spared from their usual work long enough to perform the role as audit team leader satisfactorily.

Systems programmers should be included in the team because they will have set up the system to run the way it does, and will be responsible for installing and testing any automation software that is purchased.

It is unlikely that vendor representatives would be included in a project team because they are usually too busy trying to sell solutions supplied by their company. However, vendors are often very keen to offer this kind of service.

It must also be decided whether the auditing team members are to do this in addition to their usual work, or whether they are to be taken off their usual work in order to concentrate on the audit. The first way will probably involve overtime payments for the auditors themselves. The second option will mean overtime payments for staff brought in to cover for the auditors. The first option may result in the auditors being tired when they have to audit. It can also often mean that they are distracted from their auditing role by the requirements of their fulltime job. The second option (seconded from their primary role), in most cases, is the preferred approach.

What procedure is to be adopted

The audit may be carried out completely in the open, where anyone is allowed to contribute to discussions and report what they have heard. The alternative approach is to conduct the discussion about what has been learned in rooms with closed doors.

A combination of the two techniques usually works best. An open door policy allows staff who are not part of the auditing team to know what is going on and it means that they do not feel shut out. However, a closed door policy allows the members of the committee to make suggestions for change that may be very good, without feeling that they are stepping on anyone's toes or always having to do what is best in terms of company politics.

When the automation audit begins, managers of all departments that use computer facilities should be informed. This usually takes the form of a management briefing, which can be used to explain the objectives of the audit and also the methodology being used.

It is also vital at all stages to ensure that all staff are made aware of what is being undertaken, and what the benefits will be to them of the automation.

What areas are to be audited

The usual areas to be covered in the initial audit tend to be:

- Computer room.
- Procedures.
- Media control.
- Messages.
- Schedules.
- Networks.
- User interfaces.
- Documentation.

Computer room.   There are usually a large number of manual procedures that go on in the computer room that need to be examined in great detail. Other areas closely connected with the computer room need to be investigated as well. Areas such as data preparation and tape library.

Procedures.   Most sites have procedures that must be followed under certain circumstances. Many sites have written procedures guides so that operators can look up the correct procedure in each circumstance. Some sites even have an up-to-date procedures guide. The auditors should find out what the procedures are under different circumstances, and they should also consider whether the procedure adopted is really the best one to follow, or whether some changes could be made. It is not unusual at a site to find that a particular procedure is adopted not because it is the best, but simply because things have always been done that way. It may also be possible to eliminate some procedures.

Media control. Media control refers to tapes and disks. Included in this area are the use of tape library software, automated tape systems, and, of course, System Managed Storage.

Messages. As described in Chap. 10, somewhere in the region of 80 percent of messages can be suppressed, and this is typically one of the first automation activities carried out at a site. During the audit, the number and type of messages, along with resultant actions to the system or subsystem messages, should be investigated. Also, messages from application programs should be measured in a similar way.

Schedules. Many sites have complex run diagrams that tell the operators the sequence of batch jobs to run, which order they are to be released, and their job dependencies. As described in Chap. 12, if scheduling is not currently automated, it is an area that would greatly benefit from automation software. Therefore, an audit of the current batch workload is important.

Networks. The importance of networks to the success of a company cannot be overstressed. The networks need to be audited and the use of NetView, or Net/Master (from Systems Center) considered.

User interfaces. With the move to automation, end users should have less contact with people at the data center. They should be able to use the services without wondering too much about what is happening at the other end. Where they do have contact (for example, with the Help Desk, asset management, and reports about MIS successes), it is important that these areas are audited to ensure that they perform as efficiently and as helpfully as the end user would like.

Documentation. An old style computer center will have lots of documentation around: procedures guides, printed output stored for reference, internal memos, faxes, etc.

The audit offers the opportunity to decide whether all the paper is necessary. Products such as Info/Man can be used to inform users of forthcoming, known, downtime. It can also be used to store procedures that can be viewed when the system is on line. Copies of emergency procedures to follow if the system crashes will still have to be stored on paper or on a PC.

E-mail systems can be used [DISOSS (DIStributed Office Support System) etc.] for sending memos internally, and fax gates exist for sending and receiving faxes and telex type messages. Much of the printout produced by the MIS department can be viewed on line as another method of reducing the amount of documentation. The auditors can use this opportunity to ensure that the existing documentation is correct and that a minimum of it is produced in the future.

Cost

The cost of an audit will depend on how many people are involved and for how long. To work out the cost it is necessary to decide which people are to be involved, how many days the audit is to take, and workhours total can be calculated. Knowing how much these people are paid will give a figure.

Next Steps

Once the audit is complete the next stage is to produce a report. This should include details of the way things are done now and suggestions for how they can be improved in the future. Because of the auditors familiarity with the process, they can also make suggestions for the implementation of the changes proposed.

Once the report has been circulated among senior management, a presentation should be given outlining the main points of the report and giving managers an opportunity to ask questions that may have cropped up when they read the report.

All affected staff should be given summaries of the report so that they are informed about the proposals and can voice any disquiet or make any suggestions of their own.

Once the auditors' work is done, they can hand implementation over to the team that will make the changes.

Once some of the changes have been implemented, it may be worth reauditing to find:

- How successful the changes have been.
- What future changes are necessary.
- Whether the changes are moving in exactly the right direction to maximize business efficiency.

This second audit would most likely occur two years into the project, but this will vary from site to site.

26

Automated Systems Operations and Security

Security is always a problem because most people are honest most of the time and they do not expect the hardware, software, and data that they are using to be changed in any way by anyone or anything else. Their attitude towards security is not so much apathetic as complacent. It is usually after a security violation of some kind that people start to believe in the importance of security.

It has been reported how one team of hackers waited outside a large computer installation for people to go home. The hackers posed as students researching the choice of password used by people. They asked people what their password was and why they chose it. People readily gave the information. From then on, the hackers had a wide choice of passwords to try when hacking into the system.

Large and small companies cannot afford to lose all their hardware and software. Recent surveys have shown that the majority of companies taking a hit on their computer room go out of business some time afterwards. Only companies that have alternative data centers containing up-to-date copies of files can survive successfully.

The need to secure computer-based information is therefore increasing. Large quantities of information is now stored on computer, and lots of programs are being run against it. Great damage can be done to a company commercially if its data is not secure. The reasons given for a company needing security are as follows:

- Extensive reliance is placed on computerized accountancy and record keeping.

- The operation of the company is dependent on computer-generated information.

- Computer-based systems can be extremely complex.

- Enormous difficulties and a high cost are associated with recovering from a catastrophe.

- Computer security is in the hands of a small group of people.

Therefore, management cannot ignore security risks.

The security software should run over the top of all the other automated systems operations software.

Security at a site covers the following areas:

- Restricting access to files on the mainframe computer.

- Restricting access to files on PCs and workstations.

- Restricting access to hardware.

- Restricting access to communications.

- Ensuring software is backed up.

- Ensuring that restores can be performed in a short period of time.

- Ensuring that environmental changes will not damage hardware or software.

The introduction of automated systems operations simplifies many aspects of security while creating potentially catastrophic security risks of its own.

Restricting File Access

Unauthorized access to the system is prevented by passwords. Anyone logging on from a terminal needs to know a user-id and an associated password. In the past, a list of passwords was stored in SYS1.UADS. Now security is automated with the use of RACF (IBM's access control package, now part of DFSMS) or third-party software principally from Computer Associates, such as CA-ACF2, CA-TOP SECRET, and CA-OMNIGUARD.

However, there are ways of finding out the password that goes with a particular user-id, the simplest of which is to check if someone has stuck the information on the side of the terminal.

Where users are accessing the mainframe from across a network, additional network security products can be used to prevent unauthorized access. These include such things as dial-back modems which will dial the official phone number for a user-id to be coming from.

A further level of access security can be introduced if files have a password associated with them. The would-be reader of the file needs to know the password. It is possible to have read passwords and write passwords for a file. This makes it twice as hard for someone to change data in a file.

For full security, data can be encrypted and decryption made possible only to authorized personnel. IBM's offering in this area is the Integrated Cryptographic Services Facility (ICSF/MVS).

Automated systems operations software should identify any repeated security violations so that appropriate action can be taken.

It should also be possible with automated systems operations software to prevent jobs accessing the wrong file. As systems are developed, new versions of application programs or procedures are written. With automation it should be possible to ensure that the correct version of the program or procedure is the version used by a batch job.

Restricting File Access on PCs

It is very difficult to restrict access to data on a PC. One solution is to have diskless workstations. Software is loaded on the machine from a central server and access to this server can be controlled. Files on a PC can be encrypted. PCs are susceptible to viruses if people put in infected floppy disks. It is possible to buy devices that physically block the hole for the diskette to go in. These devices can be locked and left in place.

Restricting Access to Hardware

Operators working in the computer room would notice any outsiders in there, and enquire what they were doing. However, in a lights-out area or if the computer is operated remotely, there is no one to see intruders. This means that additional physical security is required to prevent unauthorized access to hardware. This usually takes the form of pass-cards. If sites wish to install hand scanners, retina scanners, or other biometric devices, these can be linked to an automated systems operations program which would permit certain actions and take appropriate action in the event of attempted security violations.

Restricting Access to Communications

With the growth in the use of LANs and WANs, it is necessary to ensure that the data transmitted is not being received by someone else. Fiber-optic cables are much harder to break into than traditional phone lines.

Ensuring Software Is Backed Up

Traditionally, the operators would close down on-line systems and take back-ups. At weekends full pack back-ups would take place: during the week, incremental back-ups would be performed. In addition, products such as CICS would keep a journal of all changes made to the system, and applications could write output files to tape as well as to disk for added security. The operations group would also be responsible for ensuring that a copy of the back-up tapes was kept at a back-up site in case the computer room was ever destroyed or seriously damaged.

The automated systems operations software can now take on some of this role. The DFDSS component of DFSMS can be responsible for taking back-ups to tape. It is possible to transmit a copy of all changed files to a back-up site. The back-up site does not need to mirror the main site exactly because it can store the file in compressed format, and only decompress them when disaster strikes the main site.

PC and workstation users may now be running their own little data centers, that is they may be running back-ups/restores as well as installing their own software. This has security implications and the activities should be carried out by the MIS department and automated.

Ensuring Restores Are Possible

If incremental back-ups are taken over a long period of time, which can occur if on-line systems are up and running and the time available for back-ups is reduced, restoring a file can take a very long time. Typically the on-line systems are unavailable to users while this restore takes place. The ABARS (Aggregate Back-up and Recovery System) component of DFHSM can be used to restore files associated with a particular application. In the event of a serious problem, the company can be processing work using the applications that have been restored while recovery activity is being performed for other applications. The company does not have to wait until all files are restored before productive work can start. This is good news for the company that wants to remain competitive.

Environmental Protection

It is necessary to protect the computer room from fire (use of halon sprinklers), water (flood prevention), and power supply fluctuations and interruptions [usually done with a UPS (uninterruptable power supply)], batteries, and a back-up generator. Environmental monitors need to be linked to the automation software so that humans can be alerted to any significant environmental changes that occur.

Automation Software Security

When scheduler software is introduced, security software can be used to ensure that only authorized users are changing schedules, moving programs into production, querying or modifying information, and reviewing reports. Security software replaces the need for people to sign pieces of paper, and to file those pieces of paper. The security software should provide a complete audit trail.

Security administration involves using audit trails. These can be examined periodically to identify such things as usage of sensitive programs, failed log-on attempts, and the like.

The automation platform should provide a high level of security. It should ensure that all parameters that affect automation code are fully proven before each application runs.

When automation software is introduced, it is important to answer the following questions:

- Who is allowed to use the automated systems operations tool?

- Who is allowed to change operational procedures?

- Who is allowed to start and stop the automated systems operations tasks?

It is also important for management to consider what would happen if the automated systems operations tool ceased to function at any time. Someone needs to be available who knows what to do, especially if the tool could not be restarted. In the past, sites have relied on exoperators working in other departments to come back to their old jobs and run the system. As already mentioned, there are drawbacks: In the future there may not be enough exoperators to do the job; they may have forgotten much of what they knew; or the system may have changed completely (due to new procedures made available by the automation software).

My belief is that, within the next few years, the computer press will be running stories of a highly automated company that did not make its automated systems operations software secure enough. The automation software will be corrupted by unseen hands, and there will be no one watching the automation to ensure that it is working properly. By the time the company realizes what has hit it, it will be in serious financial condition and facing commercial ruin. You have been warned. Ensure that your automation software is secure and automatically monitor its performance.

27

Managing an Automated Systems Operations Environment

If an automated systems operations environment is to be established at a site, then it must be managed in the same way that all other aspects of the data center must be managed.

MIS managers are looking for tighter control over the quality of service provided by the MIS department. They also want increased productivity and performance, while at the same time enjoying the benefits of greater flexibility. The MIS manager knows that the MIS department must provide all the services required by a company to make it successful, and must provide that service at an acceptable cost.

The move to an automated systems operations environment should give managers more control over data processing. Managers need to establish service requirements and get the maximum performance out of existing resources.

There are two aspects to the management of an automated systems operations environment. First there is the management of the development of automated systems operations, i.e., managing the project team members who are introducing automated systems operations, and managing the people who are affected by the automation. Secondly there is the management of the depopulated data center environment, i.e., ensuring that the software is performing to the required standard, ensuring that service level agreements (SLAs) with end user departments are being fulfilled, making certain that procedures are in place should the automated system fail, and monitoring and reporting on the performance of the automation software.

Managing the Introduction of ASO

Project team members must be given details of the scope of the project. Perhaps more important, they must be made to realize how the automation is meant to fit in with the company's business plan, and how successful automation is meant to make the company more successful in the business community.

It is also a good idea to divide the project into achievable goals that can be used to demonstrate the success of the project to others. For example, the first activity that many sites carry out, message suppression, can usually be successfully achieved within a couple of months of the project's starting, and it demonstrates dramatically to people what achievements are possible.

The manager must not only ensure that the project team perform successfully, but also ensure that they receive praise for their successful efforts. It should be seen that senior management supports the project, and successes should be publicized so that others within the company become familiar with the scope of the project and its successes. This approach will motivate the project team to work harder towards a successful conclusion to the whole project. It will also ensure that their enthusiasm is maintained.

Managers, in association with the project team, application, and systems programmers, will have to decide on:

- Naming standards.
- Software to use.
- Procedure and standards to be followed.

While the project is going on, the manager will have to liaise with people affected by it. To begin with, this will be operators and end users. Because the initial stages in an automated systems operations project involve automated operations, it is important that the manager gets the operators involved with the project. Some operators may feel that working on the project is a way of doing themselves out of a job. The successful manager will convince them that they are vital to the success of the project as a whole, and ensure that the operators' expertise is made use of. Ways of doing this are described in Chap. 7, and the benefits to the operator of automation are described in Chap. 4. The opportunities for personal development that are available to operators with the introduction of automated systems operations are among the most compelling reasons for them to work hard towards its successful introduction.

The manager will also have to hold meetings with end users to explain how the automation project will affect them, and what benefits they will enjoy. These are also described in Chap. 4. End users will have to call the

Help Desk (if they don't already) when they experience problems. They must get out of the habit, as soon as possible, of calling operators on shift.

Managers may need to reorganize the MIS department as a whole. Traditional job areas—such as data preparation and traditional job titles, tape librarian—may no longer need to exist as separate special areas.

At every stage in the development and implementation of automated systems operations, management must ensure that the changes made can be backed out smoothly in the event of a problem, and that recovery procedures are fully tested so that they can be implemented immediately in the event of the software failing.

Managing the ASO Environment

The first requirement of a good manager is to manage people. In an automated environment there are not many people to manage, but during the process of automation and for the initial period after full automation, it is management's primary responsibility to ensure that the people taking part in the project and that the people affected by it are all performing their jobs as well and as happily as possible.

The manager's job also includes ensuring that the software installed fits the requirements of the MIS department, and will fulfill the business plan of the company. The manager, along with others involved in the automation, will have drawn up a "shopping list" of requirements for the software. Once the software is installed, it is the manager's job to check that it really meets the requirements on the shopping list. It sometimes happens that managers think that the salesperson has said that the software will perform a particular activity to a particular standard, when in fact it does not. Regular monitoring of the software's performance will involve reports (which may be produced by the automated systems operations software itself) and meetings with people affected by the change to automated systems operations. These people will have a "gut feeling" about how the new software is performing. If they are keen to come to meetings, this usually indicates they have an axe to grind, i.e., they have experienced some kind of problem or they are keen to specify improvements in the way things are done. If the software is not performing as promised, the vendor should be called in and first asked to fix the problem. If that fails, the vendor can have its software back and the company its money.

Ensuring that service level agreements are met almost always involves looking at monitor data or reports produced from that data. The reports may be produced by the automated systems operations software, or it may come from data produced by other software. The problem experienced at many sites is that an end user cannot log on to the mainframe. To the end user's mind the computer is down. However, the failing component may not be mainframe hardware, it may not be MVS, it may not be CICS, and it may not be VTAM. It may be a phone line down, it may be that the local controller has been powered off, it may even be that someone has turned the brightness all the way down on the screen. Downtime from the end user's viewpoint and downtime from the MIS department's viewpoint may be completely different. The manager must be aware of how much of the end user's downtime was due to problems with the automated systems operations software.

What is to happen at a site if the automated systems operations software fails? Is it possible to run the data center still? What procedures are to be adopted in the event of this failure? The answers to these questions depend to a large extent on how far a site is down the road to full automated system operations. Most sites have a disaster recovery plan, and many now even test the plan to see if it works. As various aspects are automated, it is important to have a plan to cope with the loss of that automation. If the message suppression/console management system fails, it could mean plugging in some old consoles and reminding operators to start jobs at specified times. If the scheduler goes, it could mean preparing an old-fashioned hand-written schedule, and scheduling some operators to work overtime through the night. Whichever part of the automation software fails, it is necessary for the rest of the automation software to identify the failure and report it to someone so that humans can take over. It is also necessary to have procedures written down so that each part of the automation can be performed by a human; for example, what commands to enter to start all the IMS regions.

The problems really come in the future when there are no operators as such. There is a person who watches a PC screen to ensure that it stays blank in the messages section, and the graph showing how busy the processor is keeps changing, but stays near the top of what it should be. There will also be some people working the Help Desk who know about operations in some detail. The other exoperators will be performing other jobs within the company. It is an unsatisfactory plan that requires the company to be scoured for exoperators to work with those still in the MIS department to ensure that a service is provided. As time passes, these exoperators will leave the company, forget what they knew, and lose touch with the latest developments. A recovery plan must be developed, and it must be examined each year to see if it is still viable. Ideally, it should also be tested.

It is important for senior management to understand exactly which areas comprise automated systems operations management. They must also keep in mind the maxim that effective management requires effective measurement.

The areas to be managed include:

- Finances.
- Messages.
- Print.
- Scheduling.
- Recovery and restart.
- Performance.
- Resources.
- Networks.
- Storage.
- Services.
- Assets.
- Security.
- Environment.

Finances

Finance management includes both outgoing and incoming flows. The days when the MIS department was able to demand money for new hardware and software in a completely ad hoc manner are gone. With good capacity planning, all changes (new CPU/training/etc.) can be planned for well in advance and the cost of the proposed changes can be included in the company budget. This way money that needs to be spent can have a less damaging effect on the overall financial well-being of the company.

Incoming flows include the price end users are charged for using the processor, storing files, using the network, printing, and for the development of applications. Managers must ensure that end users are paying a realistic price for the services they are demanding and getting.

Messages

Messages from systems, subsystems, and applications need to be managed. The automation system must deal with messages requiring responses and should suppress the others. In a situation where some operators are still employed, message automation systems might translate a system message to one that is immediately intelligible to humans, and messages could be sent to a PC. Some messages do not give enough information for an automation system to resolve a problem. In this case, the software would have to cause certain diagnostic commands to be issued to fully identify what the problem is. Where problem messages cannot be dealt with by the automation system, a problem management system must be automatically called to alert humans.

Print

As a general rule, the volume of reports produced and distributed can be reduced at most sites. Many reports are not required or at best a single page is read. Good management can be used to cut the amount of paper used, and to produce only those reports that are required. End users can look at the output on line rather than on printed paper. Other techniques, such as microfiche/E-mail/outsourcing/etc., can be used to reduce the amount of printed output produced.

Scheduling

Work to be run on the processor needs to be scheduled so that jobs are run in the correct sequence, and jobs that compete for resources are run at different times. Schedulers should actively reschedule work to optimize performance. Schedulers may even produce and test JCL. For a scheduler to function properly, the information given to it must be well managed.

Recovery and restart

Recovery and restart management means ensuring that when batch jobs or subsystems fail, appropriate steps are taken. This may involve running a separate job to back out changes that have been made to data files, or the deletion of certain temporary files, etc., before restarting the job. The scheduler must restart using the appropriate JCL and PROCs, or notify humans. In the event of a system crash, the scheduler should know what jobs it was running, and be able to restart them when the system has been restored. If the whole system has crashed, it could be the responsibility of an outboard PC or other processor to IPL the failed processor. The managers must ensure that each part of the recovery/restart jigsaw performs its assigned task and does not have a negative effect on some other part.

Performance

The operating system, i.e., MVS, and subsystems, e.g., CICS, must be monitored and managed. A monitor can simply indicate what is occurring on the system or subsystem, or it can be used to alert staff when company specified thresholds are reached, or more sophisticated software can be used to perform user-defined actions when threshold values are reached.

Management must ensure that where the software automatically performs actions, those actions will resolve the problem without creating additional problems. Management must also be sure that, when changes are made to the system or new subsystems are introduced, threshold values and auto-mated problem resolution software are modified to take account of these changes. When the software cannot overcome the problem a human must be alerted. Performance can be monitored from a screen attached to the CPU or remotely, possibly from a PS/2. The performance of the system needs to be managed to ensure that the level of service offered to clients (end users) is maintained. When performance levels deteriorate or compo-nents fail, service level agreements (SLAs) may not be met, which can have a negative impact on the success of the business.

Resources

Resource management, with capacity planning, is used to optimize what is available in terms of hardware and software (such as the number of initiators or the number of DASD designated public, etc.) and plan for future requirements. It uses values supplied by the performance monitor. Clearly, without good management bottlenecks could occur that might otherwise be avoided, and inappropriate solutions to problems could be adopted.

Networks

Users who cannot get a message from their screens to the processor because the connection is no longer available are just as unable to work as when the system crashes. Therefore, managing a network is as important to the success of a company as managing system performance. In addition, the use of remote processors increases the need for good communication management, in particular the use of PCs to IML/IPL remote processors at sites that may not have any operations personnel.

Storage

Data, programs, and JCL can often be apparently randomly placed on DASD and are often duplicated and fragmented. They may even be on non-IBM platforms. Storage managers should decide the rules that the system will follow when handling all dataset placements and deciding whether a file is to be cached. The software will also control back-ups, compaction, etc. An additional problem is the number of PCs connected via a LAN to the mainframe. Managers must ensure that data files created by the PC users are backed up automatically and can be restored when requested. Any problems must be referred to humans.

Services

Most sites have moved away from autonomous MIS departments. Now the MIS department is an integrated part of a company that offers a service to other parts of the same company or other companies. The level of service offered to clients (other departments) must be high. Managers must not only be monitoring the performance of all components of the system, but must be keeping an eye on the level of service offered to the clients. In addition, managers must be aware if end users are exceeding agreed levels of service, such as using more disk space. Real figures from performance monitor data must be used in the first place to ensure that any service levels agreed are realistic for both parties.

Assets

Asset management, which includes problem/change/configuration management, can be used to identify failing components or potential trouble spots. This can be linked with resource management. With the growth in PCs attached to mainframes, asset managers are also responsible for ensuring that all PC users who make use of an application program are using the same version and release of that program. They must also ensure that the application used is registered and not a pirated copy.

Security

Access to data and other system elements must be controlled at all times. As more activities associated with the operation of the system become automated, the fewer people there are to notice when something has been illegally accessed, modified, or deleted. It is important that access to the automation software is restricted to authorized personnel only and that any changes are fully audited.

Environment

Power supplies, temperature, and humidity all need to be controlled and fire/flood/damage alerts need to be sent in the event of problems occurring in the environment around the processor. Management needs to ensure that all contingency plans are fully tested, and that preventative measures are taken immediately once a problem is identified.

The Future

In the near automated future, the manager will have fewer people to manage, which should make management easier for him. The manager will have to ensure that the person responsible for the automation software—

i.e., the one telling the automation software how to perform—is well looked after. That person holds in his or her hands the key to the success or failure of the company.

Perhaps, in the future, the automated systems operations software will remove the need for MIS management as well.

28

Automated Systems Operations Futures

The future for many sites, in terms of automated systems operations, lies in the suggestions made in this book. Toward the end of this decade, the majority of larger MVS sites will have carried out a great deal of automation.

The Future for Operations

Hardly any messages will appear on the console, and what messages do appear will be fairly intelligible. All regular and time-dependent activities will be handled by automation software; for example, CICS will always be started at 6:00 A.M. every weekday morning (at sites that want it to). Most sites will be using a monitor and a scheduler, and these, along with the components of DFSMS, will be coordinated to optimize the performance of the data center and thereby the company. By 1997, remote operation will become commonplace for many companies that currently maintain multiple data centers. And by that time many sites will install print management software.

Sites that are further down the road to automated systems operations will be controlling multiple platforms from their MVS console. They will also be using their mainframe to automatically control the software and data files that are in use on connected PCs and workstations.

Each software platform and each subsystem has its own command format. To simplify life for the remaining operators, the automation software should have a user-friendly interface that allows the operator to tell the automation software what command they want performed and on which platform. The automation software can then enter the correct command format and point the command to the right platform and system. This could be made even simpler if a graphical user interface is involved. The operator would merely have to move the mouse and click on an icon. This would indicate the device to be affected. A pull-down menu could be used listing the commands available for that device or software.

In the immediate future, most sites will still have operators, but they will be fewer in number and much more sophisticated than traditional operators. They will not be at the beck and call of the machine but will be more in control of it. It is likely that for large parts of the day there will be no operators in the computer room, but they will be able to dial in from a PC if the automation software pages them to tell of a problem. Many operators will move to the Help Desk area which will gain in status and prestige and become more "intelligent" in its ability to fix end user problems, which, because of the automation software, should be fewer anyway.

It is quite likely that the job title of operator will disappear and what remains of the operator's role will be performed by people with a different job title as just a part of their overall role within the company.

Improvements in the sophistication of automated operations software are being announced all the time.

The Future for Data Center Design

In the future, data centers themselves will be redesigned. Areas for staff will no longer be required, but space should be allocated for automatic hardware, and a lot of thought will need to be given to security considerations.

The Future for End Users

In the future the life of the end user will be much simpler. They will not need to understand JCL or know about blocking sizes or storage media. SMS will automatically manage the placement of data for them, as well as back-ups, restores, and archiving. The introduction of the Information Warehouse framework means that the end user will not have to worry about which format was used to store data or even on which computer platform the data resides.

The end user will be able to tell the scheduler software when batch jobs are to be run and will be able to view the results from a terminal.

The use of PCs and workstations by end users attached to the mainframe by LANs or WANs is growing. In the future, far more MIPS will be on the desktop in the form of PCs and workstations than in the MIS department. This means that there will be an increase in distributed data and client-server applications.

At present, PC users may be running their own little data centers; that is, they may be performing back-ups and restores, and installing software. This has security implications. In the future the activity will be taken over by MIS and automated.

Automated PC software distribution can save a company millions. Most sites have many PCs that are not properly managed. Who knows what release of DOS, OS/2, MS-Windows, or Lotus 1-2-3 is on each machine? Who knows how the memory is configured, or whether the hard disk can accommodate the new application? This makes asset management hard. It makes installation of updates to software very hard. Products such as Network Navigator from Annatek automate the software distribution process. Applications are sent from the host to the PC, appropriate system files on the PC are amended, and status reports are sent back to the mainframe.

The Future for Application Programmers

In the future, new software purchased by a company will be automatically downloaded from the supplier's computer. The software will be automatically installed. Fixes and updates for the software will be automatically downloaded and automatically installed.

In the future there will be a great deal of convergence of software. Despite the fact that Computer Associates seems to be buying out all the other software suppliers, there are still a large number around and each piece of software has its own characteristics. It is likely that in the future software from all vendors will be easier to install, maintain, and use. It is likely that mainframe software will, like software on the Apple Macintosh, have a common user interface, irrespective of the supplier it is from. It is also likely that the software will expect the user to be working with a mouse or some other pointer device.

Currently, up to 80 percent of programmer's time can be spent testing and debugging existing systems. An Automated Testing Tool (ATT) could improve the overall quality of an installation, and free up programmers' time for other work. The future is likely to see a growth in the availability and use of ATTs.

An ATT should identify the following potential software errors:

- Problems with logic.
- Calculation problems.
- Inability to handle bad data.
- Poor coding techniques.

- Hardware or software constraints.

- Inadequate capacity planning.

Every branch in a program should be tested after each change.

After a failure it is necessary to see a formatted dump or start an interactive debugger. It is better if this can be done without exiting from the ATT.

The suggested characteristics for an ATT are:

- Ability to capture and reexecute transactions from multiple terminals and different VTAM environments.

- Ability to provide an unattended and batch compare facility independent of script, including both file and terminal data.

- Provide standard and consistent commands and menu structure.

- Scripts maintained easily (editor).

- Directly interface to security packages.

- Integrate with other tools.

- Reexecute without having to manually restore files.

- Handle full range of testing: unit, concurrency, integration, regression, stress, and acceptance.

The Future for System Programmers

The future may not only see a lights-out computer room, but a lights-out systems programmer area. The current level of system programmers' technical specialization may not be required in the future. If much of a systems programmer's time is spent installing packages and ensuring that the packages run with the other packages that are installed, and writing user exits to ensure the software works to the site's requirements, it is possible for the work to be carried out by the software vendor. The vendor will provide the systems programmer level of expertise, and this will be included in the price. When a piece of software is selected, the vendor will sell it, install it, ensure that it runs, and maintain it.

There are many instances where problems occur with software or hardware, or changes (typically upgrades to the latest release) need to made to existing software. Automation in the area of asset (problem/change) management is not particularly straightforward. Some hardware and software vendors now maintain an on-line database of known faults, and, wherever appropriate, known fixes. In the future it would be possible to automatically dial a company's database and search it for a solution to a problem experienced at a site. If none is found, the hardware or software vendor's staff could access a company's mainframe and run their own diagnostics remotely. They could identify the cause of the difficulty and suggest a way of fixing it. If it is software, it would be possible for the vendor to download the appropriate code to fix the problem.

Typically, a site will, from time to time, modify its hardware configuration. Older hardware will be replaced, new types of hardware will be introduced. Currently, someone has to decide where on the computer room floor devices are going to stand. Someone has to ensure that appropriate files [such as IOCDS (input output configuration dataset)] are told about the devices existence, and what addresses they are located at.

The move to automated system operations will, hopefully in the near future, allow hardware devices to be connected to the network without tables needing to be updated, or an IPL performed.

Capacity planning is usually concerned with ensuring that resources available are fully utilized, and ensuring that in the near future there will be enough system resources to meet the requirements of the user population. Data used by capacity planners is collected by system monitors. The capacity planners take the data and draw graphs, carry out what-if? analysis, etc.

In the future, more sophisticated software could be used that would perform most of the tasks carried out by capacity planners. Programs that run on mainframes and PCs are both currently available, and improvements in their speed, reliability, and output can be confidently anticipated. This will reduce the man-power required.

The Future for Management

With the introduction of automated systems operations it is possible that in the future the management of the MIS department can be automated. There will be no operators or people working in jobs peripheral to operations, therefore no one to manage. Reports, etc., that have to be sent to other departments could be produced automatically. The person who controls the automation software will be the only one left in the MIS department, and perhaps his role too can be automated.

Certainly, the management aspects of SystemView show the way that IBM sees the management of a data center evolving. With the introduction of products that conform to SystemView, mainly from third-parties, it is possible to automate the SystemView managements and eventually aspire to a lights-out MIS managers office.

Selecting Automated Systems Operations Software

Introduction

When selecting automated systems operations software, it is useful to first draw up a list of requirements. Each requirement can be assigned a weight. The automation products under review can then be tested against the list of requirements. An overall "score" for each product can then be obtained. No two sites will necessarily come up with the same "winner" because different sites will weight the requirements differently.

A word of warning: Many people don't know what they want until after they have made the wrong choice.

This appendix suggests some questions that a company may find it useful to ask vendors when purchasing automated system operation software. The main automation products generally fit into one of the following categories:

- Host and networking.
- Job schedulers.
- Report distribution tools.
- Storage management tools.
- Environmental tools.

Questions

General questions

What are the unique product features?

How many product licenses are there worldwide?

How long has the product been available?

List price	Processor group	Purchase	Annual rental
	40		
	50		
	60		
	70		
	80		
	other		

What are the software requirements?

What are the hardware requirements?

Does the product have its own security system?

- If yes, please specify:
- No

What is the typical installation time (excluding customization)?

What is the typical implementation time to create a usable system?

What are the staff requirements (in workhours) for implementation?
    System programmers
    Operations analysts
    Operators

What are typical resource consumption figures (as a percentage) for running the product to perform significant automation activities on an ES/9021 340?

For host and network products

Which of the following are supported by the product?
    Message suppression and rerouting.
    Reply to console messages.
    Time-of-day event triggers.
    Automated "catch-up" processing.
    Message-driven tasks.
    Automated system/application start-up/shutdown.
    Automated system/application recovery.
    Automated problem notification.
    Support for unattended operations.
    Remote operations.
    Heterogeneous operations.
    Network alert detection anywhere in the network.
    Heterogeneous network environment.

What type of "automation languages" does the product offer?
    Procedural (own proprietary).

Procedural (nonproprietary, e.g., CLIST, REXX, PL/I etc.).
Rule based.
Other (please specify).

Does the product offer facilities to improve the operator console interface?

If yes, what form does this improvement take?
ISPF-like interface.
Operator workstation concept.
SAA CUA.
Other (please specify).

What testing facilities are offered?
Operation in report only/warning mode.
A simulation environment.
An event tracing facility.
Other (please specify).

Can ASO strategies be modified/changed in a nondisruptive manner?

What mechanisms are available to support message text independence?
Message parsing facilities.
Status variables derived for the message.
Other (please specify).

What interfaces exist to other products?
Within and outside the company's product line?

What "drop-in" applications are supplied?

Are products "ready to use" or more starter set/tool kit in form?

What facilities/interfaces exist to allow users to interface to their own applications?

What RAS features are built into the product?

Is external automation facility, such as an outboard PC, available?

If yes:
Is it integrated with the host-based facility?
Does it interface to heterogeneous hardware platforms?
Is it capable of unattended/automatic system IML/IPL?
Does it offer a remote interrogation facility?
Does it support dial-out tone/message pager facilities?
Is voice support supplied?
Is voice/touch tone response supported?

How does the product integrate with/support other installation management disciplines, such as:
Performance monitoring/tuning?
Environmental management?

Problem/alert management?

Other (please specify)?

Can internal functions be fully controlled by an external security package?

For job schedulers

What method of job tracking does the product employ?
SMF feedback.
Output processing.
JES intercepts.
Systems hooks.
Other (please specify)

Does the product require system hooks (e.g., SVC, Appendage)?
If yes, what are they?

Must the product run from, or have entries in, an authorized library?

Does the package integrate with a report distribution system without user modifications?

Does the package integrate with a restart/recovery package without user modifications?

Does the product require dedicated JES classes?

Does the product run on JES3?

Does the package fully perform on all versions of MVS?

If an overnight schedule is currently running, can the following modifications be made without running batch jobs?
Changes in priority.
Changes in resource usage.
Addition of jobs.
Deletion of jobs.

Can optional jobs be placed in the middle of a set of dependencies without the need to modify the database each time the job is run, other than the requesting of the job itself?

Which systems can access all the on-line functions of the package?
CICS.
TSO.
IMS.
Roscoe.
Other (please list).

How many, if any, resource types does the package track to prevent resource contention?

What calendar scheduling criteria are available?
Daily.
Specific day of the month.
Specific day of the year.
Other (please specify).

How many other events may trigger job submission as a standard feature of the supplier's product?

In which systems can events be tracked without user modification?
NetView.
IMS.
Other (please specify).

Can the product perform the following?
Step level condition code checking.
Status checking other than via COND codes or abends.
"Abend is ok" logic.

Can internal functions be fully controlled by an external security package?

For report distribution tools

What method of report collection does the product employ?
External writer collection.
JES subsystem interface.
JES intercepts.
Systems hooks.
Other (please specify)

Does the product require system hooks (e.g., SVC, Appendage)?

If yes, what are they?

Must the product run from, or have entries in, an authorized library?

Does the package integrate with a job submission system without user modifications?

Does the product require dedicated report classes?

Does the product run on JES3?

Does the package fully perform on all versions of MVS?

Are JCL modifications mandatory to run any part of the product?

Can JCL listings (JESLOG, etc.) be managed by the product?

What systems, if any, can be used to view reports on line (e.g., CICS)?

Is report bundling available as a standard feature?

Is report archiving available as a standard feature?

What type of database holds the reports?
Spool.
VSAM.
Database.
Other (please specify).

Can print collection directly input to the database without going via spool?

What compression algorithm does the product use?
Trailing space truncation.
LZW.
Huffman.
Proprietary.
Other (please specify).

What percentage compression can an average user expect to achieve?

How is final print processing achieved?
Batch jobs.
Print sub-system supplied with product.
On-line system with report spin-off.
Other (please specify).

Does the product consolidate the archiving medium as a standard feature?

Can internal functions be fully controlled by an external security package?

For storage management tools

Which of the following does the product provide:
Data migration/recall.
Data archiving.
Incremental back-up/recovery.
Volume back-up/recovery.
Support for remote operations.
Support for heterogeneous environments.
Support for automated storage management at remote sites.
Support for automated storage management at unattended sites.
Remote site recovery initiated at central site.
Complete automation of periodic storage management function.

Which data formats/dataset organizations does the product support?

Is retrieval of migrated/archived data automatic (or transparent) to end users, or must they perform an explicit act to recover data?

How are storage management policies defined to the product?

Via parameter definitions.
Via exit modules/ customization modules coded in a high-level language.
Via exit modules/ customization modules coded in Assembler.
Other (please specify).

Can storage management policies be modified dynamically?

What user interface is provided to the product?

Does the user interface conform to SAA guidelines?

What interfaces exist to other products
Within the supplier's own product line?
Outside the supplier's own product line?

What facilities/interfaces exist to allow users to interface to their own applications?

Does the supplier's product provide facilities for the complete automation of periodic storage management functions?
If yes, what are they?

What storage management functions is it currently not possible to automate with the product?

Can internal functions be fully controlled by an external security package?

For environmental tools

Which of the following can be monitored/controlled?
Air conditioning units.
UPS systems.
Security alarms.
Fire alarms.
Temperature sensors.
Water detectors.
PDU circuit breaker.
MG sets.
Other (please specify).

What input sensors are supported?
Digital.
Analog.

How many input sensors are supported?

What output interfaces are supported?
Digital.
Analog.

How many output interfaces are supported?

Can multiple monitoring units be networked together?

Is it possible to consolidate/base decisions on input across separate units?

Automated Systems Operations Software Packages and Suppliers

The following is a list of the automation products available for use with MVS. While every attempt has been made to ensure that the list is as complete as possible, it is quite likely that some products have been omitted.

In Section 1, products have been grouped under the general heading for their principal function. Section 2 contains the names, addresses, and telephone numbers for these suppliers.

Section 1

Automated console response systems

ACC (Automated Command Center)	Tone Software
AF/OPERATOR	Candle Corporation
AF/REMOTE	Candle Corporation
ASAp	Cognitive Data Systems, Inc.
AUTO-ANSWER	StarTech Software Systems, Inc.
AUTOMATE	Legent Corporation
Automatic Operator	Infolink Software, Inc.
AutoOperator	Boole & Babbage
CA-OPERA	Computer Associates
COMENSA	Votek Systems Ltd.

COMMAND MVS	Macro 4
CONMAN	Jason Data Services, Inc.
CONSOLE/MASTER	Mantissa Corporation
CONTROL-O	4th Dimension Software
DOCS	Smartech Systems, Inc.
FAQS	Goal Systems
Logical Console Operator	Netec International, Inc.
LOGOUT	Macro 4
MVS CO-PILOT	Cybermation, Inc.
Natural Console Management	Software AG
NetView	IBM
ODDS/MVS	Software Engineering of America
OPS-MASTER	Mantissa Corporation
OPS/MVS	Goal Systems
RASP	AYDE Software Solutions, Inc.
SYS/MASTER	Systems Center
WTO-MANAGER	Empact Software
ZACK	Altai Software, Inc.

Print management software

$AVRS	Software Engineering of America
BETA92	BETA Systems Software, Inc.
BETA93	BETA Systems Software, Inc.
BIMSPOOL	B I Moyle Associates
BUNDL	Legent Corporation
CA-DISPATCH	Computer Associates
CICS/SPOOLER	MacKinney Systems
CICSPRINT	Macro 4
CMA-Spool	Symark International
CONTROL-D	4th Dimension Software
CPF	Software Technology, Inc.
DTA/PRINT	Davis, Thomas & Associates
EXPRESS	Goal Systems
INFOPAC	Mobius Management Inc
Natural Output Management	Software AG
OMC (Output Management Center)	Tone Software
PAGEZERO	Information Systems Assist Co.

RMDS (Report Management & Distribution System)	IBM
RMS (Report Management System)	Mantissa Corporation
SAR	Goal Systems
SPEEDVIEW	Cybermation, Inc.
Spool Manager	Infolink Software, Inc.
TRMS	Software Engineering of America
TS-RMDS	Tone Software
VIEWCOM	StarTech Software Systems, Inc.
VTAMPRINT	Macro 4
WSF2	RSD America
X/PTR	Systemware
ZINA	Altai Software, Inc.

Schedulers

ASAp	Cognitive Data Systems, Inc.
ASF	Chaney Systems, Inc.
CA-7	Computer Associates
CA-SCHEDULER	Computer Associates
CONTROL-M	4th Dimension Software
CSAR	Software Engineering of America
ESP (Execution Scheduling Processor)	Cybermation, Inc.
INFOPAC	Mobius Management, Inc.
JOB-MASTER	Mantissa Corporation
JOBTRAC	Goal Systems
OPC/A (Operations Planning and Control/Advanced)	IBM
PJS plus	Advanced Data Management, Inc.
Smart/Scheduler	Pecan Software
SPANEX	DBSE Software, Inc.
THE BOSS	Mobius Management, Inc.
ZEKE	Altai Software, Inc.

Automated rerun recovery software

CA-11	Computer Associates
CONTROL-R	4th Dimension Software
P ENCORE	Cybermation, Inc.

RUN.MASTER   Mantissa Corporation
ZEBB   Altai Software, Inc.

Job control software
BETA77   BETA Systems Software, Inc.
CA-JCLCHECK   Computer Associates
DSF (Dynamic Support
  Subsystem)   Chaney Systems, Inc.
JOB/SCAN   Diversified Software Systems, Inc.
JCLCLEAN   Software Engineering of America
JCLPREP   Altare Computer Software

Automated report balancing and control
BETA91   BETA Systems Software, Inc.
Smart/CC   Pecan Software
U/ACR   Unitech Systems, Inc.

Disk space abend software
STOP-X37   Empact Software

Tape management system
CA-1   Computer Associates

Tape dataset stacking utility
TDSU   U.S. West

Automated problem management system
MECO   Software Engineering of America

Access control packages
ALERT/MVS   Goal Systems
Blockade   Cybermation, Inc.
CA-ACF2   Computer Associates
CA-OMNIGUARD   Computer Associates
CA-TOP SECRET   Computer Associates
RACF   IBM

Help Desk software

PC-based software

Brock Activity Manager Series	Brock Control Systems, Inc.
CBR Express	Inference Corporation
Clientele	AnswerSet Corporation
CSS	Strategic Microsystems Corporation
Dominion	InterApps, Inc.
Expert Advisor	Software Artistry, Inc.
First Class	AI Corporation
Help/Desk	Coastal Technologies
Help Desk Expert Automation Tool (HEAT)	Bendata Management Systems
Helpdesk-1	Coastal Technologies
Help Desk Expert Automation Tool (HEAT)	Bendata Management Systems
Helpdesk-1	AST/The Data Corporation Group
Help Express	Software Marketing Group, Inc.
Infotrak	Trident Software
KBMS	AI Corporation
MGV HelpDesk	MGV Computer Consuling, Inc.
Napa	Peregrine Systems
Openup Time	MCSS, Inc.
Phoneserver/Distributed Call Center	Unifi Communications Corporation
Problem Management Productivity Services (PMPS)	IBM (PS/2)
Professional Help Desk	Legent
Quetzal Software	Corporate Software, Inc.
Right Tracker	Mushroom Software
ServicePoint	Service Point Development Corporation
Support Express	Software Marketing Group, Inc.
Support Magic	Magic Solutions
Support Wise	Business Wise, Inc.
Top of the Mind	The Molloy Group
Topic Intelligent Document Retrieval System	Verity, Inc.
Utopia	Hammersly Technology Partners, Inc.

Mainframe-based software

CA-Netman	Computer Associates
ESP-ELS	Enhanced Software Products, Inc. (VM)
Impact	Allen Systems Group
Info/Man (Information/Management)	IBM
Keys	Software Engineering of America
Multitrack Work Request System	Multitrak Software Development Corporation
PNMS III	Peregrine Systems
PRISM	Cincom Systems
Program Management Extended (PMX)	

Automated performance management

AF/PERFORMER	Candle Corporation

Automated systems monitors

ALERT/MVS	Goal Systems
Blockade	Cybermation, Inc.
CA-LOOK	Computer Associates
CMF	Boole & Babbage
MICS	Legent Corporation
Omegamon	Candle Corporation
Resolve Plus	Boole & Babbage

Network monitors

NetView Performance Monitor	IBM
NetSpy	Legent
Omegamon II for VTAM (Omegacenter)	Candle Corporation
The Monitor for VTAM	Landmark
Vital Signs for VTAM	BlueLine Software

Network automation software

Automator "mi"	Direct Technology
DREAM	Grand Metropolitan
High-Level Language Application Programming Interface (HLLAPI)—PC options	IBM
Net/Master	Systems Center
NetView	IBM

Other AO products

CA-UNIPACK	Computer Associates
CO-OPERATE/1	Andersen Consulting
EPIC/Auto-Op	Goal Systems
MAINVIEW	Boole & Babbage
Natural Operations	Software AG
OMEGACENTER	Candle Corporation

PC Software

Automator	Direct Technology (NY)
The Intelligent Console	Votek Systems Ltd.
Watch-It	Operations Control Systems

Inventory control packages for PCs

Cluster	Touchstone Software Corporation
LAN Automatic Inventory	Brightwork Development, Inc.
LAN Directory	Frye Computer Systems, Inc.
LAN Auditer	Horizons Technology, Inc.
Network HQ	Magee Enterprises, Inc.
Monitrix	Cheyenne Software, Inc.

Section 2

The following is a list of the company names and addresses mentioned above.

4th Dimension Software, Inc.
3176 Pullman Street
Suite 116
Costa Mesa, CA 92626
USA
(714) 755-7855

Advanced Data Management, Inc.
15 Main Street
Kingston, NJ 08528
(609) 799-4600

AI Corporation
130 Technology Drive
Waltham, MA 02154
(617) 891-6500

Allen Systems Group, Inc.
750 11th St South
Naples, FL 33940
(813) 263-6700

AnswerSet Corporation
21771 Stevens Creek Boulevard
Cupertino, CA 95014
(408) 253-7515

AYDE Software Solutions
24 Highway 213
Covington, GA 30209
(404) 786-1686

Altai Systems
624 Six Flags Drive
Suite 150
Arlington, TX 76011
(817) 640-8911

Altare Computer
8921 Murray Avenue
Gilroy, CA 95020
(408) 842-1114

Andersen Consulting
100 South Wacker Drive
Chicago, IL 60606
(312) 580-0069

AST/The Data Group Corporation
177 South Bedford Street

Burlington, MA 01803
(617) 272-4100

Bendata Management Systems
1755 Telstar Drive
Suite 101
Colorado Springs, CO 80920
(719) 531-5007

BETA Systems Software
111 Anza Boulevard
Suite 412
Burlingame CA 94010
(415) 344-4014

B I Moyle Associates, Inc.
5788 Lincoln Drive
Minneapolis, MN 55436
(612) 933-2885

BlueLine Software
Suite 690
5775 Wayzata Boulevard
Minneapolis, MN 55416
(612) 542-1072

Boole & Babbage, Inc.
510 Oakmead Parkway
Sunnyvale, CA 94086
(408) 735-9550

Brightwork Development, Inc.
766 Shrewsbury Avenue
Jerral Center West
Tinton Falls, NJ 07724
(908) 530-0440

Brock Control Systems, Inc.
2859 Paces Ferry Road
Overlook 111, Suite 1000
Atlanta, GA 30339
(404) 431-1200

Business Wise, Inc.
595 Millich Drive, Suite 210
Campbell, CA 95008
(408) 866-5960

Candle Corporation
Commerce Plaza

2001 Spring Road
Oak Brook, IL 60521
(312) 954-3888

Cheyenne Software, Inc.
55 Bryant Ave
Roslyn, NY 11576
(516) 484-5110

Cincom Systems, Inc.
2300 Montana Ave
Cincinnati, OH 45219-2418
(513) 662-2300

Coastal Technologies
615 Valley Road
Upper Mont Claire, NJ 07043
(201) 744-3338

Cognitive Data Systems
701 Pinebrook Drive
Lombard, IL 60148
(708) 495-1110

Computer Associates Int, Inc.
711 Stewart Avenue
Garden City, NY 11530
(516) 227-3300

Corporate Software, Inc.
275 Danbird Road
Canton, MA 02021
(617) 828-7727

Cybermation, Inc.
16 Esna Park Drive
Markham, ON
Canada L3R 5X1
(416) 479-4611

DBSE Software
PO Box 61686
Houston, TX 77268
(713) 440-7091

Direct Technology
10 East 21st Street
Suite 1204/5
New York, NY 10010
(212) 475-2747

Diversified Software Systems
18630 Sutter Boulevard
Morgan Hill, CA 95037
(408) 778-9914

DTA, Inc.
505 N Highway 169
550 Waterford Park
Minneapoli͏, MN 55441
(612) 591-6100

Empact Software
1803 Overlake Drive
Conyers, GA 78209
(404) 483-8852

Enhanced Software Products, Inc.
1 Hollis Street
Wellesley, MA 02181-9766
(617) 235-3518

Frye Computer Systems, Inc.
19 Temple Place
Boston, MA 02111
(617) 247-2300

Goal Systems International
7965 N. High Street
Columbus, OH 43235
(614) 888-1775

Grand Metropolitan IS
5 Country View Road
Malvern, PA 19355
(215) 296-3838

Hammersly Technology Partners, Inc.
250 Montgomery Street, Suite 710
San Francisco, CA 94104
(415) 956-1300

Horizons Technology, Inc.
3990 Ruffin Road
San Diego, CA 92123-1826
(619) 292-8320

Inference Corporation
550 N Continental Boulevard
El Segundo, CA 90245
(310) 322-0200

Infolink Software, Inc.   .
1400 Fashion Island Boulevard
Suite 603
San Mateo, CA 94404
(415) 574-3305

Information Retrieval Companies, Inc.
312 West Randolph, suite 610
Chicago, IL 60606
(312) 726-7587

Information Systems Assistance Co.
105 Wallie Court
Garner, NC 27529
(919) 779-6054

InterApps, Inc.
610 9th St., Suite 3
Hermosa Beach, CA 90254
(310) 374-4125

Jason Data Services, Inc.
22661 Lambert Street Suite 206
El Toro, CA 92630
(714) 770-7789

Landmark Systems Corporation
8000 Towers Crescent Drive
Vienna, VA 22182-2700
(703) 893-9046

Legent Corporation
Two Allegheny Center
Pittsburgh, PA 15212
(412) 323-2600

MacKinney Systems
2740 S Glenstone
Suite 103
Springfield, MO 65804
(417) 882-8012

Macro 4, Inc.
Brookside Plaza
PO Box 187
Mount Freedom, NJ 07970
(201) 895-4800

Magee Enterprises, Inc.
PO Box 1587
Norcross, GA 30091
(404) 446-6611

Magic Solutions
180 Franklin Turnpike
2nd floor
Mahwah, NJ 07430
(201) 529-5533

Mantissa Corporation
201 Summit Parkway
Birmingham, AL 35209
(205) 945-8930

MCSS, Inc.
20975 Swenson Drive, Suite 160
Waukesha, WI 53186
(414) 798-8560

MGV Computer Consultant, Inc.
10 Bay Street, Suite 700
Toronto, Canada M5J 2R8
(416) 362-2257

Mobius Systems, Inc.
One Ramada Plaza
New Rochelle, NY 10801
(914) 632-7960

The Molloy Group, Inc.
40 Malapardis Road
Morris Plains, NJ 07950
(201) 267-4464

Multitrak Software Development Corporation
119 Beach Street
Boston, MA 02111-2520
(617) 482-6677

Muchroom Software
PO Box 360451
Strongsville, OH 44136
(216) 225-0844

Netec International
PO Box 180549
Dallas, TX 75218
(214) 343-9744

Operations Control Systems
560 San Antonio Road
Palo Alto, CA 94306
(415) 493-4122

Pecan Software Corporation
419 East Crossville Road
Suite 107
Roswell, GA 30075
(404) 594-9707

Peregrine Systems
1959 Palomar Oaks Way
Carlsbad, CA 92009
(619) 431-2400

RSD America, Inc.
100 Merrick Road
Suite 500E
Rockville Center, NY 11570
(516) 536-8855

*Service Point Development
Corporation*
210 West 200 North, Suite 101
Provo, Utah 84601
(801) 373-3859

Smartech Systems, Inc.
10015 W Technology Boulevard
Dallas, TX 75220
(214) 956-8324

Software AG
11190 Sunrise Valley Drive
Reston, VA 22091
(703) 860-5050

Software Artistry, Inc.
3500 Depauw Building, Suite 1100
Indianapolis, IN 46268
(317) 876-3042

Software Engineering of America
2001 Marcus Avenue
Lake Success, NY 11042
(516) 328-7000

Software Marketing Group
108 3rd Street, Suite 106
Des Moines, IA 50309
(515) 284-0209

Software Technology, Inc.
1511 Park Avenue
Melbourne, FL 32901
(407) 723-3999

StarTech Software Systems, Inc.
80 Beaver Street & Wall Street
 Court
New York, NY 10005
(212) 943-9800

Strategic Microsystems Corporation
1661 Route 22 W
Bound Brook, NJ 08805
(908) 356-2121

Symark International, Inc.
5655 Lindero Canyon Rd
Suite 502

Westlake Village, CA 91362
(818) 889-0978

Systems Center
1800 Alexander Bell Drive
Reston, VA 22091
(703) 264-8000

Systemware, Inc.
12770 Coit Road
Suite 1008
Dallas, TX 75251-1306
(214) 239-0200

Tone Software Corporation
1735 S Brookhurst Street
Anaheim, CA 92804
(714) 991-9460

Trident Software
1001 Bridgeway, suite 104
Sausalito, CA 94965
(415) 332-0188

Touchstone Software Corporation
2130 Main Street
Suite 250
Huntington Beach, CA 92648
(714) 969-7746

Unifi Communications Corporation
4 Federal Street
Billerica, MA 01821
(508) 663 7570

Unitech Systems, Inc.
3030 Warrenville Road
Suite 600
Lisle, IL 60532
(312) 505-1800

US West
1999 Broadway
Room 1140
Denver, CO 80202
(303) 896-6062

Verity, Inc.
1550 Plymouth Street
Mountain View, CA 94043-1230
(415) 960-7600

Votek Systems
4880 Blazer Memorial Parkway
Dublin, OH 43017
(614) 761-8688

Bibliography

Books

Automated Operations in an IBM MVS Installation, Protocol International, 1988.
Automated Operations Packages, Xephon plc, 1992.
Carico, Bill, *Automated Operations: Accepting the Challenge*, ACTS, 1991.
Data Center Strategies for IBM Users, various authors, Xephon plc, 1991.
Miller, Howard W., *How to Automate Your Computer Center: Achieving Unattended Operations*, 1990, QED Information Sciences Inc.
MVS Automated Operations Software, Xephon plc, October 1989.
Output Strategies for IBM Users, various authors, Xephon plc, 1991.
Seadle, Michael S., *Automated Mainframe Management: Using Expert Systems with Examples from VM and MVS*, McGraw-Hill, 1991.
The IBEX Bulletin (monthly publication), Xephon plc.

Articles

Davis, Dwight B., "IS Automates for Data Center Survival," *Datamation*, November 1990.
"Expert System Advisors Slow Getting to Market," *Software Magazine*, March 1991.
Francis, Bob, "The PC's Role in Mainframe Control," *Datamation*, August 1990.
Milliken, Keith, "Expert Systems in the Automation of Systems Operations," *Mainframe Journal*, July 1990.
"'MIS in 'Radical Change,'" *Software Magazine*, January 1991.
Myers, Scott, "Console Automation Software," *Mainframe Update*.
Osmundsen, Sheila, "At Automation Fork, Paths Lead to MVS or Outboard PCs," *Software Magazine*, January 1991.
"Report Distribution Systems," *Mainframe Update*, June 1991.
Schare, Marc, "MVS Automated Operations Systems," *Enterprise Systems Journal*, May 1991.

Glossary

3278 A monochrome terminal that attaches to a 3274 controller.

3330 Old removable disk.

3340 Old removable disk.

3420 9-track reel-to-reel tape drive.

3480 Cartridge tape drive.

3490 A smaller rack-mounted version of the 3480.

3495 Tape library dataserver, i.e., an ATL.

37xx Family of communication controllers. They are the boxes that go between the mainframe channel and the modems and phone company.

3800 Laser printing system. It uses fanfold or rolls of paper and prints quite fast.

ABARS Aggregate Back-up And Recovery Support is part of DFHSM. It allows all the files associated with a specific application to be grouped together. This allows them to be restored together so that work can be performed by end users while restore activities are continuing.

ACA Automated Console Application is associated with ISCF under NetView and allows remote 3090 processors to be controlled.

ACF/VTAM Advanced Communication Function/Virtual Telecommunications Access Method is a multihost version of VTAM.

ACO Automated Console Operation, part of NetView SolutionPac. It has now been superseded by AOC/MVS.

AConnS Application Connection Services allows an OS/2 user connected to a mainframe to use mainframe facilities.

ACS Automatic Class Selection is a DFSMS facility allowing automated control of dataset placement.

AFP Advanced Function Printing—IBM's way of getting the best out of laser printers and reducing the size of the spool files necessary to achieve this.

AI Artificial Intelligence is the name given to software that tries to emulate human thinking.

AIX Advanced Interactive eXecution is IBM's version of Unix.

ANO Automated Network Operations is part of NetView SolutionPac and is designed to automate network operations procedures. It has been superseded by ANO/MVS.

ANO/MVS Automated Network Operations/MVS is the replacement for ANO in NetView SolutionPac. It automates many aspects of network operations.

AOC/MVS Automated Operations Control/MVS replaces the NetView subtask ACO. It offers similar facilities of automating operator functions at a console.

API Application Programming Interface allows users to "connect" one piece of software to another.

ATL Automatic Tape Library allows cartridge tapes to be taken from a library (usually a silo) by a robotic arm and loaded.

ATM Automatic Teller Machine is used by banks as a way of offering customer service out of hours.

ATT Automated Testing Tool can be used to thoroughly test application programs before they go into production.

BCS Basic Catalog Structure contains information about VSAM and non-VSAM datasets on a disk.

BMP Batch Message Processing is an IMS region.

BTAM Basic Telecommunications Access Method is an old communications software program. It does not support SNA devices and has been replaced by VTAM.

CDRM Cross Domain Resource Manager is an SNA component that is used in multidomain environments.

CEC Central Electronic Complex is the name given to a collection of processors that present a single system image to end users.

CICS AO/MVS Customer Information Control System Automation Option/MVS can be used to automate many of the activities previously carried out by the CICS operator.

CLIST Control list of interpreted instructions can be used to control sequences of events. The more powerful REXX is likely to supersede it.

CNM Communications Network Management refers to the interfaces and entities that make up the SNA network management architecture.

CNMI Communications Network Management Interface is a VTAM interface that allows an NCCF command processor to request and receive network management information from a network.

CPU Central Processor Unit is the part of the computer that actually does the work, i.e., it does the adding up.

CUA Common User Access is part of SAA and specifies the ways in which the user interface to systems is to be constructed.

DASD Direct Access Storage Device is almost always a disk pack.

DB2 DataBase 2 is an IBM-produced relational database management system.

DCB Device Control Block is part of JCL. It can be use to specify blocksizes, record formats and logical record lengths.

DCMF/MVS Distributed Change Management Facility/MVS allows software installation on unattended PCs in a network.

DFDS Data Facility Device Support is old software that has been incorporated into DFP.

DFDSS Data Facility DataSet Services is the MVS back-up and recovery software. It is part of SMS.

DFEF Data Facility Extended Function is old software that has been incorporated into DFP.

DFHSM Data Facility Hierarchical Storage Manager is designed to manage dataset migration and recall. It is part of DFSMS.

DFP Data Facility Product is a necessary component of MVS. It handles catalog management and access methods. It is part of DFSMS.

DFSMS Data Facility Storage Management Subsystem is a way of managing data stored. Its component products are DFP, DFDSS, DFDSS, RACF, and DFSORT.

DFSORT Data Facility sort is IBM's sort utility. It is part of DFSMS.

DIDOCS Device Independent Display Operator Console Support is an old method of controlling messages and operator consoles.

DISOSS DIStributed Office Support System is an office automation product that runs under MVS. It is meant to have been replaced by OfficeVision/MVS.

DRDA Distributed Relational Database Architecture is IBM's standard for communicating with SAA-distributed databases.

DXT Data eXTract is a utility that allows data to be extracted from a database.

E-mail Electronic mail is a way of sending memos from one user's screen to another, thus saving paper.

EDA/SQL Enterprise Data Access/Structured Query Language provides data access within the Information Warehouse.

ESCMS ESCON Monitor System can be used by a central site to control devices at a remote site.

ESCON Enterprise System CONnectivity refers to the high speed fiber-optic channels that can be connected to mainframes.

ESDS Entry Sequenced DataSet is a VSAM sequential file.

GMF Graphic Monitor Facility can be used with NetView to monitor network performance from a graphic workstation.

Help Desk A single point for end users to contact when they require help or information that is not available from any other source.

ICF Integrated Catalog Facility is the name given to the MVS catalog structure. Its component parts are BCS and VVDS.

ICSF/MVS   Integrated Cryptographic Service Facility/MVS is the software that allows data files to be encrypted.

IDRC   Improved Data Recording Capability is IBM's way of improving the storage capacity of 3480 cartridge tape drives.

IML   Initial Microcode Load is the process, usually associated with power on, when machine level instructions are loaded into the hardware.

IMS   Information Management System is a transaction processing system similar to CICS.

IMS AO/MVS   IMS Automation Option/MVS performs routine operator functions including starting of IMS regions automatically.

Info/Man   Information Management is an IBM facility that allows information to be stored and retrieved on line.

IOCDS   Input Output Configuration DataSet specifies which devices are connected to the mainframe.

IPL   Initial Program Load is the name given to the process of loading the first program into the mainframe's memory. By extension, it is also used to apply to the whole process of bringing up the software that is permanently running, e.g., VTAM, CICS, etc.

ISC   Inter-System Communication is used between host applications using LU6.2 protocols.

ISCF   Inter-System Control Facility is a NetView application that allows remote operation of processors.

ISMF   Interactive Storage Management Facility allows users to specify the data classes, management classes, storage classes, and storage groups to be used at a site. It is part of SMS.

ISPF   Interactive System Productivity Facility runs under TSO and offers end users a menu-driven system to perform their work.

JCL   Job Control Language is used to specify the programs and datasets that are to be used.

JES   Job Entry Subsystem is a generic term for the MVS batch processing subsystem.

JES2   Job Entry Subsystem 2 is typically used at sites with fewer batch jobs.

JES3   Job Entry Subsystem 3 is usually used by sites with large amounts of batch work to perform.

KSDS   Key Sequenced DataSet is a VSAM indexed dataset.

LAN   Local Area Network is a network used to connect PCs and workstations.

LU   Logical Unit is the way that users get into an SNA network.

LU6.2   Logical Unit 6.2 allows peer-to-peer networking in an SNA environment.

MCS   Multiple Console Support is an MVS feature that allows more than one operator console attached to the system.

MIPS Million Instructions Per Second is a way of measuring processor power. It is not always considered to be a suitable unit.

MIS Management Information Systems is the name given to the department that controls the running of the computer.

MPF Message Processing Facility is a very basic MVS message management system.

MRO Multi-Region Operations allows multiple copies of CICS to be run concurrently.

MSU Management Service Units are used by NetView to improve automated responses to messages.

MVS Multiple Virtual Storage is IBM's flagship operating system for large systems.

MVS/ESA MVS/Enterprise Systems Architecture is the latest version of MVS. It improves performance by using hiperspaces and dataspaces.

MVS/SP MVS/System Product is the base MVS system.

MVS/XA MVS/eXtended Architecture first offered 31-bit addressing as a way of improving performance.

NAU Network Addressable Unit is an entity in an SNA network that can send and receive requests and responses. Examples of entities are SSCP, LU, and PU.

NCCF Network Communication Control Facility is now part of NetView. It provides network operator control facilities.

NCP Network Control Program is an SNA program that runs in the communications controller. It performs much of the work necessary to control a network.

NetView NetView is now IBM's vehicle for controlling and managing automated operations as well as network operations.

NLDM Network Logical Data Manager is now part of NetView. It collects session statistics.

NPDA Network Problem Determination Application is now part of NetView and called Hardware Monitor. It collects and displays error statistics for network components.

NPM NetView Performance Monitor uses VTAM to monitor the performance of SNA and Token Ring networks.

NPSI NCP Packet Switching Interface is a way of connecting X.25 networks to SNA networks.

NVDM NetView Distribution Manager controls the distribution of data and software among processors in an SNA network.

OCCF Operator Communication Control Facility allows remote systems to be controlled from a host over an SNA network.

ONMA Open Network Management Architecture is IBM's OSI architecture.

OPC/A Operations Planning and Control/Advanced is a suite of programs designed to automate batch work.

OPC/ESA   Operations Planning and Control/Enterprise System Architecture is a better version of OPC/A offering more in the way of expert systems.

OS/2   Operating System /2 is deigned to run on the PS/2.

OSI   Open System Interconnection is an international set of communication standards.

PARMLIB   Parameter library used to specify system parameters to the MVS system.

PC   Personal Computer—IBM's microcomputer that has been heavily cloned.

PDM   Print Distribution Management is an alternative name for an RDS. It looks after the printing or not of output produced on a mainframe.

PDS   Partitioned DataSet is a file made up of a number of members. The members are themselves sequential datasets. SYS1.PARMLIB is an example of a PDS.

POS   Point-of-Sales terminals can input data directly to a mainframe for use in a variety of programs.

PR/SM   Processor Resource/System Manager offers a way of logically partitioning a processor.

PS/2   Personal System /2 is IBM's business-oriented personal computer.

PTF   Program Temporary Fix is a correction to a bug in the software.

PTT   Post, Telegraph, and Telephone administration is the generic name for phone companies in different countries.

PU   Physical Unit is an SNA component that controls the communication hardware in a node.

QMF   Query Management Facility is an SQL-based query and report writing system. It is an end user tool.

RACF   Resource Access Control Facility is IBM's access control system. It is part of DFSMS.

RAID   Redundant Arrays of Inexpensive Disks are disk drives containing a large number of small platters and heads.

RDS   Report Distribution System is the type of software that looks after the printing and distribution of reports.

REXX   Restructured EXtended eXecutor is an SAA procedural language. It is very powerful and easy to use. It replaces CLISTs.

RRDF   Remote Recovery Data Facility is a facility available with CICS, DB2, and IMS, which allows recovery data to be logged to a remote site.

SAA   Systems Application Architecture is meant to provide a consistent user interface to all applications.

SDLC   Synchronous Data Link Control is a high-speed data synchronous data transfer protocol.

SDSF   System Display and Search Facility is used at JES2 sites to monitor the progress of work through the system.

SLA   Service Level Agreement is used to ensure that the end users are expecting the level of service that the MIS department can provide.

SLR   Service Level Reporter will report on system performance.

SMA   System Management architecture is a name for the architecture behind SystemView.

SMF   System Management Facility collects data on MVS system activity which can be used for accounting and capacity planning.

SMP/E   System Modification Program /Extended is a method of upgrading or modifying the MVS system.

SMS   System Managed Storage is IBM's plan for storage management. It is implemented by products in the DFSMS family.

SNA   Systems Network Architecture is IBM's communications architecture.

SNI   System Network Interconnection allows dissimilar SNA networks to exchange information.

Spool file   Jobs waiting to start and print files waiting to print are stored in an area called the spool, and are referred to as spool files.

SQL   Structured Query Language is a standard language for accessing information in a relational database.

SSCP   System Services Control Point exists within VTAM and handles network name/address conversion, device configuration, network diagnostics, and recovery.

SSI   SubSystem Interface is internal to the MVS operating system. It allows messages to be passed from one subsystem to another or to MVS.

SSNT   SubSystem Name Table is a PARMLIB member that includes the name of the subsystems that can use the SSI.

Syslog   The system log keeps a record of all system messages and commands.

SystemView   SystemView is the SAA-approved structure for managing an Enterprise system.

TCP/IP   Transmission Control Protocol /Internet Protocol is a set of protocols for networking data.

TIRS   The Integrated Reasoning Shell runs under OS/2, MVS, and other systems. It is an expert system with a variety of applications.

TSCF   Target System Control Facility is a NetView automation facility. It allows remote operation including IML and IPL.

TSO   Time Sharing Option is the MVS time sharing system. It allows users to sit at terminals and work interactively.

UPS   Uninterruptable Power Supply is used to ensure power continues to be supplied to a processor even after the main supply is hit.

VM   Virtual Machine is IBM's hypervisor operating system which allows just about any other operating system and subsystem to run under it.

VNCA   VTAM Node Control Application is network management software and is now part of NetView.

VSAM   Virtual Storage Access Method is IBM's integrated file storage system. It allows indexed files, sequential files, and direct access files to be stored in special datasets.

VSE   Virtual Storage Extended is IBM's operating system for medium-sized and small sites.

VTAM   Virtual Telecommunications Access Method is mainframe resident software which manages session establishment, and data flow between terminals and applications or applications and applications.

VTOC   Volume Table of Contents is resident on disk packs and contains information about all non-VSAM files and VSAM areas stored on the disk.

VVDS   VSAM Volume DataSet contains information about VSAM datasets stored on a disk.

WAN   Wide Area Network is the generic name for a network that goes over a large area and needs to conform to CCITT standards.

WORM   Write Once Read Many is the term for devices that are used as permanent repositories of data.

X.25   X.25 is the international standard for attachment to packet switched networks.

XMS   Cross Memory Services is used to connect two NetViews so that messages can pass from one to the other.

XRF   EXtended Recovery Facility is available with CICS and IMS providing recovery on a mirror-image system in the event of the primary system crashing.

YES/MVS   Yorktown Expert System/MVS is an attempt to schedule batch work, manage JES queues, report incidents, and monitor performance. It requires VM.

Index

About the Author

Trevor Eddolls is a senior consultant who edits the internationally acclaimed *VM, VSE,* and *VSAM Updates,* published by Xephon, a U.K.-based research organization. In addition he has produced many user surveys including *MVS Automated Operations Software* and *The Help Desk in Practice,* and he has contributed articles to a number of technical publications. He has lectured extensively throughout the U.K., Europe, and the Middle East on many aspects of mainframe computing, and has recently spoken at a U.K. VM User Group meeting, the UKCMG, and has chaired a VM/VSE Futures seminar. Trevor Eddolls is the author of *VM Performance Management,* also published by McGraw-Hill.